Darcy La

CW00551823

Darcy Lange: Study of an Artist at Work

Edited by Mercedes Vicente

Irish Roadworkers, 1971

Foreword

Rhana Devenport, Director, Govett-Brewster Art Gallery
Jonathan Watkins, Director, Ikon

Darcy Lange: Study of an Artist at Work examines the practice of
New Zealand video pioneer Darcy Lange and is associated with the
exhibition of the same title held at the Govett-Brewster Art Gallery in
2006, curated by Mercedes Vicente. Lange (1946–2005) was born in
Urenui, Taranaki, Aotearoa New Zealand, his practice encompassed
video as well as sculpture, photography, film and flamenco music.
In 1972 he had begun videotaping and filming under the general
theme of 'people at work' in English factories and mines. Soon
after, he returned to New Zealand and continued documenting
workers' lives in Taranaki, and during the late 1970s, Māori activists'
struggles to establish land rights from Bastion Point to Ngatihine,
north of Auckland. In 1976–7 he embarked upon his important
video project in Birmingham and Oxfordshire, *Work Studies in
Schools*. Guy Brett notes that Lange adopted video as a means of
involving himself "with real people and real problems of life".

Thematically, 'people at work' situates Lange's practice
within a lineage of social documentary film and photography and
a shared ideological genealogy dating back to 1930s American
FSA (Farm Security Administration) photographers Dorothea
Lange and Lewis Hine. With these seminal works, he became one
of the first artists to incorporate the 'long take' in the recording
of people's actions in real time as they performed daily working
tasks. His restless experimentation with the structural possibilities
of the moving image and the still image, led to a parallel use of
photography, film and video, simultaneously shot.

The capacity for early portable video to provide live and taped
feedback – unlike film or photography – meant it could serve as a
medium for criticism and analysis, and a catalyst for social change.
Lange stressed the relationship with the subjects of his recordings
by playing back the recorded material to them. In his work studies
in Birmingham and Oxfordshire schools, Lange recorded teachers
in the classrooms, then the teachers' and the students' reactions to
the tapes. The absence of electronic editing equipment in the early
stages of video, which prevented shaping a tape into a finished
product, further encouraged the development of a 'process' video

aesthetic. Lange never conceived of these tapes as finished works but as "researches" and "an educational process". The reactions of his subjects to the tapes became part of the body of work, guiding him in its development. By exposing the process, Lange's videos become in themselves studies of videotaping as a work activity.

For this first major publication dedicated to Lange's practice, Mercedes Vicente presents a pivotal account of Lange's life, work and activism, and his vital contribution to the expansion of video as a medium. Art historian Benjamin H. D. Buchloh examines the history of documentary photography and conceptualist video in order to locate Lange's dignifying portrait of labour as a foil to globalised consumerist artistic culture. London-based critic and curator Guy Brett engages with Lange's work in light of current directions in screen-culture and recent decades of performance and its documentation. He pays particular attention to the possibilities, so harnessed by Lange in the 1970s, of the 'new' media of video, especially his early use of the 'long take' and his handling of playback as a component in the pedagogical process in *Work Studies in Schools*. Brett's 1977 introduction to the *Work Studies in Schools* catalogue is reproduced here in full; this text was originally published by the Museum of Modern Art Oxford, whose then director David Elliott commissioned the project from Lange. Film writer Lawrence McDonald examines Lange's work in relation to documentary and ethnography, using the Birmingham schools project and the origin of cultural studies as an historical and theoretical background. Photographer and close collaborator of Lange's John Miller and media studies commentator Geraldene Peters further focus on Lange's *Māori Land Project* in relation to video/film practices as well as activism concerning Māori land rights during the late 1970s and 1980s in Aotearoa New Zealand. Pedro G. Romero addresses flamenco as a "tool for survival and a way of life". He moves further to discuss Lange's devotion to flamenco guitar and his teacher and guide, Diego del Gastor of Morón de la Frontera in Spain. Conceptual artist Dan Graham delivers a personal eulogy, addressing Lange's interest in flamenco music, and their shared engagement with community and social justice concerns. Graham's is a reminiscence of Lange's politicisation and avant-gardism from which he draws a parallel – interestingly as does Buchloh – to Courbet. A description of works and a chronology posit these discussions within the wider scope of Lange's oeuvre.

Lange's connection with the Govett-Brewster in Taranaki began 40 years ago in 1968 when his early abstract sculptural work was acquired by the inaugural director John Maynard and subsequently exhibited in 1970 in the opening year of the gallery. In 1985 a major retrospective of his work occupied the entire gallery, while in 1983 his entire videography to that date was acquired. He then performed at the gallery in both 1986 and 1998, and his video works were included in group exhibitions at the gallery in 1998 and 2004. Ikon's' 2008 exhibition in Birmingham, *Work Studies in Schools*, offers an important opportunity to examine Lange's project at this moment, three decades later, within the historical and social context of its making.

This publication marks a commemorative collaboration as Ikon hosted Lange's first one-man exhibition in the UK in 1971. It was also in Birmingham where he produced his first video *Breakers Metalworks* (1972) and *Study of Three Birmingham Schools, UK* (1976) as part of the *Work Studies in Schools* presented in this exhibition following its restoration.

We would like to sincerely thank Mercedes Vicente for her dedication to the recovery of Lange's work within an international context and for the thorough research she has tirelessly undertaken since 2005 in relation to a serious and systematic reappraisal of the artist's video and archival material. Through her efforts, Lange's archive is now at the Govett-Brewster while his video material, housed primarily at the New Zealand Film Archive, is more accurately and fully archived, documented and considered. This primary research has been invaluable to the process of bringing to light the artist's practice within an historical and theoretical framework, emphasising Lange's contribution to and role within the history of video and media arts.

We would also like to thank Helen Legg for her collaborative efforts towards the 2008 Ikon exhibition and for undertaking significant new research associated with Lange's *Work Studies in Schools* in Birmingham. This would not have been possible without the generosity of Creative New Zealand.

Appreciation is extended to all those who have supported and assisted this vast and ongoing project, especially to the Lange family, particularly Darcy's children Darcy and Rawinia, his former wife Maria Snijders and his brother Roger Lange.

Rhana Devenport & Jonathan Watkins

Jack Jury, Stockman, Uruti, Taranaki, 1974

Preface

Mercedes Vicente

> Nothing that has ever happened should be regarded as lost
> for history … To articulate the past historically … means
> to seize hold of a memory as it flashes up at a moment of
> danger. Only that historian will have the gift of fanning the
> spark of hope in the past who is firmly convinced that even
> the dead will not be safe from the enemy if he wins.
>
> Walter Benjamin [1]

These words, quoted by Dan Graham in his introduction to
Darcy Lange's memoir *Video Art*, resonated so pertinently in this
belated publication, a manuscript that had languished since
the early 1980s before publication in 2001. By then, amidst the
editor's genuine intentions of giving Lange a fair place in the
history of video practices in New Zealand, the amendment simply
had come too late for the artist and his career. Beyond the initial
effect of soothing Lange's wounded confidence, the book might
have nurtured in him aspirations of long overdue recognition in
New Zealand (and abroad as it was Lange's wish to promote the
book overseas with the aid of financial support that he was never
granted). *Video Art* was received with silence and suffered similar
obscurity to that of its manuscript, which had sat in a box for nearly
two decades. Ironically, the book went out of print after Lange's
death, when the retrospective at the Govett-Brewster Art Gallery in
2006 reclaimed his overlooked career.

Many different circumstances conspired to make this
exhibition and catalogue possible: that Benjamin H. D. Buchloh
suggested I seek out Lange's work once in New Zealand; that
Lange was from Taranaki, the same region as the Govett-Brewster
Art Gallery where I was heading, and that he died a month after
my arrival. From there a chain of correspondences drew me to
his work, including my interest in video and film of the 1970s,
and his social and political activist commitment. Some of these
connections were personal such as Lange's love for flamenco and
my native Spain, and our shared understanding of geographical
displacement and the fracturing of identity that results. We shared
this desire to 'seize hold of a memory' and record those who would

1   Walter Benjamin, as quoted in Dan
    Graham's introduction to Darcy Lange,
    Video Art, The Department of Film,
    Video and Media Studies, University of
    Auckland, Auckland, 2001, p. 5.

otherwise be obscured by history. All of which drew me to the work of Lange – and that is ultimately serendipitous. Too pragmatic to believe in fate, I have rather crudely accepted the turn of events leading to this fortunate encounter, and I am grateful that luck was on my side to embark on such a significant project.

Lange had an urge for legitimation, as artists do. In his works, his ultimate aims were to communicate and engage with the world. Perhaps that is why in his later years he favoured his flamenco guitar playing, which in the Antipodes provided him with a (small) community. "Loneliness and art", he once wrote, "are strange things – it is different in music. I have fewer worries with music, my other love." [2]

Lange had some qualms, however, about both videotaping his subjects and his motivations for doing so, saying:

> ... making videos and photography in other people's areas, as I have done with my art – whether it be walking in their area, entering their houses, absorbing their ideas or recording them on their burial grounds or their places at work – was due to many motives, not all good, I must say – at times it was for my career, at other times in search of a new image for art. But these motives were balanced by the reciprocal respect that caught me as I entered other people's territories, as I explored those people so they explored me, and we changed together. [3]

These concerns mirror my own about resurrecting Lange from the history of video art in New Zealand and internationally. Balancing these also is the hope that the exhibition and this accompanying publication will effect the reception and re-evaluation of Lange's work; perhaps inspiring contemporary and future artistic practices.

The preservation of Lange's work and archives has been an important feature of this project. The impermanent nature of video appealed to artists in the 1970s; offering a challenge to the art market, and causing many video works to be 'written out' of history. As Chris Meigh-Andrews remarks:

> the history of video art, unlike the history of painting and sculpture, cannot be rewritten with reference to 'seminal' or canonical works, especially when those have disappeared. It is also obvious that videotapes that are not considered 'significant' are unlikely to be preserved, archived or restored. [4]

2   Ibid., p. 8.

3   Darcy Lange as cited in the brochure of the exhibition 'Land Work People, Darcy Lange Survey', Govett-Brewster Art Gallery, 1985.

4   Chris Meigh-Andrews, *A History of Video Art: the Development of Form and Function*, Berg, Oxford; New York, 2006, p. 5.

The recent conscious efforts to rescue this medium from its material disappearance are not fortuitous, but rather a dual exercise of preservation and legitimation. Lange might well have shared the fate of many fellow video practitioners as Meigh-Andrews describes, perhaps afflicted by the geographical isolation of his relocation to New Zealand in 1984; fading away from the context that had sustained his early career.

With Lange's entire oeuvre now held on permanent loan at the New Zealand Film Archive where it will be preserved; with the creation of the Darcy Lange Archive held at the Govett-Brewster; and with this publication; the immediate moment of danger is past and Lange's contribution to the history of video will be available for future historians.

It may be legitimate to ask: what (and for whom) are the ultimate benefits of this endeavour? And, with what sort of authority and critical position have I been entrusted in order to orchestrate this shift in the reception of Lange's work in New Zealand and internationally? David Curtis once wrote: "Often in this history, success for an individual has depended upon the existence of the critical mass of a group of sympathetic peers." [5]

We, the contributors to this book, are this group. We hope that it might attract those who might have lost sight of Lange, as well as assist the next "critical mass" who will sustain his legacy into the future.

5   David Curtis, *A History of Artists' Film and Video in Britain*, British Film Institute, London, 2007.

*Studies of Teaching in Four Oxfordshire
Schools, UK*, 1977

Julia Swift at Banbury School.

Study of an Artist at Work

Mercedes Vicente

> … making videos and photography in other people's areas, as
> I have done with my art – whether it be walking in their area,
> entering their houses, absorbing their ideas or recording
> them on their burial grounds or their places at work – was due
> to many motives, not all good, I must say – at times it was for
> my career, at other times in search of a new image for art. But
> these motives were balanced by the reciprocal respect that
> caught me as I entered other people's territories, as I explored
> those people so they explored me, and we changed together.
>
> Darcy Lange [1]

Darcy Lange's video practice, and by extension his early use of
photography and film, could arguably belong to the tradition of
social documentary given its social and political referent and his
aspirations of raising awareness and potential agency for his subjects.
It should, however, be taken into account that as a pioneer of video,
the origins and development of Lange's practice parallels that of
the medium itself. To examine it one must also trace Lange's formal
training as a sculptor and his early attention to the intrinsic qualities
of representational media. His shift towards the mechanical media of
image production can be attributed to his a desire to record, rather
than recreate, and later to engage with, the subjects he portrayed.
Lange perceived these media as instruments for social reality, able
to establish a more objective understanding of social relations.

Lange's commitment to realism and his concern with issues
of 'truth' and objectivity were paramount in his early work. It led to
his parallel and simultaneous use of photography, film and video
and to the exploration of the boundaries of these media – concerns
he shared with the structuralists yet rarely became his prime focus.
When Lange later adopted video exclusively, the interaction with
the subjects that he portrayed and its potential to effect social
and political change became predominant. By the end of the
1970s, starting with the *Māori Land Project* (1977–80), Lange's
attention had evolved towards the examination of dominant modes
of representation, looking at video as a tool for political action
outside the confines of institutionalised television.

1   Darcy Lange as cited in the brochure
     of the exhibition *Land Work People,
     Darcy Lange Survey*, Govett-Brewster Art
     Gallery, 1985.

2   *Formality I*, 1967.

Extended Formality I, 1967.

3   Darcy Lange in an interview with
     Willoughby Sharp, *Avalanche*, Summer
     1975, p. 12.

Formative Years as a Sculptor and Transition to Photography and Film

A graduate of Elam School of Fine Arts in Auckland, New Zealand (1964–7), and The Royal College of Art in London (1968–71), Lange was trained as a sculptor. His transition to video occurred in 1972 after an initial encounter with photography and film, working with all three media simultaneously in his early projects until he finally adopted video as his only medium. At the time, the shift to video from sculpture may have seemed a natural one for artists willing to engage with more overtly social content. This move surfaced within the context of a shift in the art discourse towards the radical 'dematerialisation' of the object that rendered the purely formal language of sculpture futile and unengaged. This sentiment was shared by other contemporaries of Lange trained in sculpture, such as New Zealand artist Leon Narbey and British artist David Hall, who went on to become film-makers and video artists.

While a student at Elam School of Art, Lange worked in large, bold abstract geometric steel constructions characteristic of the late 1960s. [2] Lange had originally attended Elam to study music but found it too academic, and instead opted for the sculpture department. Structure and composition were central to his studies and Lange showed interest in Bellini, Vermeer, Cézanne, Brancusi and Mondrian. He was introduced also to the work of photographers Dorothea Lange and Edward Weston who proved to have a lasting influence on his video work. At the Royal College, his sculpture practice began a gradual shift towards realism. There, he included figurative elements to the abstract geometric structures. Lange described his transition as: "Hard edge, three dimensional steel Mondrian things. And then in London, I moved gradually into realism, or representationalism, moving that composition back into a Vermeer thing, where it's hidden under the structure of the work". [3] Tableaux of human figures with painted backdrops referencing New Zealand landscape eventually gave way to incorporating photography in the form of slide projections. This approach culminated with his graduate thesis work *Irish Roadworkers* (1971), [4] later exhibited at Ikon Gallery in Birmingham in his first solo exhibition in the UK. A scene of Irish road workers repairing Oxford Street in London was recreated with life-size figures surrounded by four screens of projected slides showing the street traffic (two of the carousel projectors operated with dissolve units to mimic movement). This last sculptural work is the key to understanding Lange's shift to photography and film. It also marks the beginning of Lange's commitment to the subject of 'people at work'.

The desire to reproduce reality rather than recreate it is what determined Lange's move away from sculpture. As he explained: "Then I thought it's just ridiculous reconstructing people in the round; it seems obvious that you should literally present them as they are. And what's the best way to do that? Film and photography."[5] These sculptural figures were renditions, with verisimilitude, of the Irish workers whom Lange had photographed at the site. Thus, the step from using photography as a referencing tool to the use of photography to reproduce the actual subject would seem a logical one, especially within the context of the prevailing conceptualism of the era and the notion of the 'dematerialisation' of the object. It is relevant to note that this is the only sculpture that Lange included in his list of video, film and photographic work, referring to it as a 'sculpture reconstruction' and alluding to the slide projections as independent studies in their own right. Lange attributed this transition as having been "influenced by the growing conceptual art movement, and the falling away of the restrictions of the Royal College, plus the continuation of my interest in the subject of work, and the desire to bring out class difference in British society".[6]

The British video art scene came about as a consequence of, among other contributing factors, the development of accessible video technology and the rise of minimal and conceptual art. As David Hall has identified, against other historical accounts, early video art in the UK derived from a conceptualist rather than a formalist approach, which he claimed was separated from much of the film making of the late 1960s and early 1970s. Hall wrote that, in retrospect, early British video works owed "more to conceptualist rather than formalist concerns. This important (though often confused) distinction was what, as well as its production and display systems, separated it not only from current obsessions in the mainstream plastic arts but also from formalist avant-garde film of the time with which it has often been identified. Conceptualism was intended as a liberation from the shackles of the object and consequently its filmic counterpart (preoccupation with materiality), encouraging for some a potential for greater social engagement".[7] In this respect, Hall's argument frames Lange's relationship to conceptualism, as it serves to explain

4   *Irish Roadworkers*, 1971.

5   Lange, ibid., p. 12.

6   Lange, ibid., p. 12.

7   David Hall, 'Early Video Art: A Look at a Controversial History' in *Diverse Practices: A Critical Reader on British Video Art*, Julia Knight (ed.), Arts Council of England and John Libbey, 1996.

8   *Craigdarrock, Scotland*, 1973.

9   Darcy Lange, *Video Art*, The
      Department of Film, Television and
      Media Studies, Auckland University,
      Auckland, 2001, p. 37.

10   Raymond Feddeman and Truke
      Van Koeverdam (eds.), *Darcy Lange
      Māori Land Project*, Stedelijk Van
      Abbemuseum, Eindhoven, Netherlands,
      and Internationaal Cultureel Centrum,
      Antwerp, Belgium, 1980, p. 33.

11   Lange, *Avalanche*, p. 12.

12   Ibid., p. 12.

13   Conversely, flamenco would come
      to represent and offer the antithesis
      to his Calvinist convictions, released
      from its coercive influence for being
      considered part of leisure. Although
      one of Lange's projects which never
      materialised was titled *A Study of the
      Art of Flamenco as Work*.

14   *Social Consideration, Communication
      and Observation*, 1971.

Lange's leap from sculpture to video. The fact that he exhibited in the early 1970s at Jack Wendler Gallery in London along with artists like Sol LeWitt, Joseph Kosuth and Lawrence Weiner clearly identifies his affiliation with this artistic scene. However, Lange's ultimate commitment to the social subject and the documentary mode of representation, geared towards his interest in labour and the class system in the UK, clearly separated him from these artists, and thus explains his critical and often ambivalent position in regards to these conceptual practices. In a statement referring to his video *Craigdarrock* (1973),[8] a study of a day's work among shepherds in Scotland, he wrote: "In some ways the videotape was a satire of a Richard Long walk that I had seen on film, and I must say it was and perhaps is one of the truest balances between conceptual art and a documentation of actual work or social reality".[9] In 1980, when asked where he stood in relation to conceptual art, his response was categorical: "I don't especially want to talk about that aspect. To me conceptual art means getting the concepts right."[10]

For Lange, the topic of work initially arose as a way to address issues of the class system in the UK that he was confronted with upon his arrival in London from the more egalitarian New Zealand society. Being a Marxist, the theme of work in regards to the issue of class was a political one for Lange, and one that carried with it ideological implications. He stated: "… by the time of the last year at college, my work was no longer a quiet observation. It was becoming more aware in a political sense and more concerned with social commentary".[11] Furthermore, speaking of *Irish Roadworkers*, he traced his ideological roots to Maoist art, "I think it was social realism in an almost classic sense, quite influenced by Maoist art".[12] The roots of Lange's engagement with the subject of work could also be found in his father's Calvinist heritage. One could argue that his Calvinist work ethic may have been at odds with his choice of becoming an artist, thus, the need for art to be seen, or be, like 'work' to find its justification.[13]

In 1971 Lange produced his first series of six super-8 films, under the title *Social Consideration, Communication and Observation*,[14] recording for the first time in moving image people conducting work activities. These included a woman putting out her washing in London, a hardware store employee in South Kensington, farmers burning off wheat in Kent, a man milking cows in Sussex, a cattle auction in a market outside Bradford, and a transport café in London. These short, three to eight minute films, were unedited, single-takes, accompanied by a soundtrack played on a tape recorder. Along with the films, Lange shot his subjects in black and white still photographs and in colour slides. Lange conceived these films as "a prolonged still photograph", like capturing a pose held over a few minutes, and "coming out of the three-dimensional era of presenting a moment in time". [15] They were an extension of a form of portraiture he started with his *Irish Roadworkers* and earlier figurative sculptures realised at the Royal College.

Lange stressed the need for art to engage with life and the world around us, seeing art as a communicative tool and the artist's role as a catalyst to raise social consciousness. He declared: "I am involved in the development of a social conscience, and a development of a record and a memory of the physical world. Art seems to have become so isolated ... Because of the need to understand, there is a need to communicate". [16] And this, according to Lange, was precisely where abstraction failed to succeed and justified his reason to adopt representation and representational media.

This series was followed by *Studies of Family Groups* (1972), [17] where Lange examines eating habits across different class groups, choosing a middle class family and working class family in London (originally there was a third study of a farming family that was never conducted). These half-hour long, 16mm films with synchronised sound were "natural observations", intended to exhibit traits about society, personalities and mannerisms. [18] As in the previous works, the reference to still photography is prominent. The films were more structured and show the first attempt at consciously making a comparative study across classes through the careful selection of subjects. Lange also devised a systematic camera technique: the first eight minutes are a long shot with a fixed frame then the camera zooms in gradually and follows the conversation and the actions of the subjects, returning to its original composition for the last eight minutes. On this occasion Lange again photographed his subjects using colour slides and black and white film, although he never exhibited these photographs. The use of photography continued to feature in later works, whether photographs were exhibited alongside the films and videos or were considered as part of the 'final work'.

15   Darcy Lange, *Video Art*, p. 13.

16   Ibid., p. 20.

17   *Studies of Family Groups, UK*, 1972.

18   Darcy Lange in Rosetta Brooks, *A Survey of the Avant-garde in Britain*, Gallery House, London, 1972, vol 3, p.24.

Video and the Documentation of People at Work or *Work Studies* 1972–7

The cost of film stock and associated technical difficulties was a major setback for Lange who had to borrow equipment from the Royal College after he graduated. He also depended on his cameraman, New Zealand film-maker Rodney Charters and New Zealand photographer Alyson Hunter (his partner at the time, who also did most of Lange's photographic work until 1974).

Phil Slight, a New Zealand painter who taught in the School of Art Education in Birmingham, introduced Lange to video and lent him his equipment. It was in Birmingham in 1972 that Lange made his first videotape, *Breakers Metalworks*, as part of the series *Five Working Studies in British Factories and Workplaces* (1972–3) [19] which marked the beginning of Lange's factory observations. These studies were conducted mostly in factories located in East London (where Lange resided at the time) and in Leicester and Birmingham (where he worked), and included a clothing manufactory, a knitting factory, a woodcarving furniture workshop and a metal works factory.

Here the recording style was that of a walk-through of the factory with a roaming hand-held camera that aimed to convey, through a prosaic lens, the atmosphere and realities of factory life. It also included some footage of the workers' leisure time. These raw recordings, of poor visual and audio quality, look tentative and preliminary when compared to later works such as *A Documentation of Bradford Working Life* (1974). As Lange became more acquainted with the use of the video camera and gained experience with the narrative nature of moving image, he developed a more systematic approach in his work. He began to focus more succinctly around particular subjects and their respective activities, through a careful selection of different types of labour and the assigned (and repetitive) tasks carried out by an individual or in working groups. *Five Working Studies* served as a study for the later Bradford series and set Lange's seminal style of real-time, unedited, unmediated, long observations of people at work that came to characterise his *Work Studies* series (1972–7).

Five Working Studies was exhibited by Sigi Krauss and Rosetta Brooks as part of a number of avant-garde exhibitions hosted at Gallery House in London in 1972. John Du Cane, in the catalogue of the exhibition, remarked how Lange's *Breaker Metalworks* struck him "as a good example of video used for what it's best at: situation

19 *Five Working Studies in British Factories and Workplaces*, UK, 1972.

Study of an Artist at Work

retrieval". He wrote: "Lange conveys the full immediacy of the factory work with no mediation by commentary or interview. His subjective response – gentle and curious – as cameraman, and the workers' playful acceptance of his presence makes it a powerful personal communication of a specific social activity." [20]

Lange continued using photography and film simultaneously with video, exploring the intrinsic qualities of all three media in works such as *A Documentation of Calverton and Pleasley Coal Mining Communities, Nottingham, UK* (1973) [21] and his Bradford series, before he abandoned this exercise altogether, shifting to video exclusively. In *Coal Mining Communities*, for example, he experimented with video's synchronised sound and the 'wild' or ambient sound of his 16mm film, exhibiting both at the same time. He also emphasised the 'objecthood' quality of the film equipment, devising dramatic displays of metre-long loops of 16mm film that drew attention to their sculptural qualities. These formal exercises should not, however, be seen as the sole intent. Above all, what prevailed was a straightforward display of all three media, side by side, as three representational modes of documenting the same subject.

What permeates Lange's interest in working across multiple media (regardless of embracing all as parts of the 'final work') is his intention to examine and convey the subject matter in its most 'truthful' way by offering multiple renditions of the same material with the subtle variations introduced by the intrinsic qualities of each medium. There is an implicit recognition of the limitations and the impossibility of fully conveying reality by any one of these means. It is evident that Lange's examination of these three media transcended the pure formal exercise, as Lange insisted on the issue of 'truthfully' recording reality, and being at the service of the subject he portrayed. In this respect, Lange, in an interview with Willoughby Sharp, conceded the lasting influence of photographer Tom Hutchins, who taught him at Elam, "whatever happens in front of the camera is what makes what you do with the camera valuable". Lange continued: "this is the way you translate what you see outside, the way you present it. It's an entry device. It's a way of making things accessible. It has to do with communication". [22] Sharp replied by coining it "a structured eye". [23] Structure therefore becomes for Lange an objective device at the service of his observational activity; it is a way to organise the reality that he aimed to document through drawing a pre-established order.

20   John Du Cane, *A Survey of the Avant-garde in Britain*, p.2.

21   *A Documentation of Calverton and Pleasley Coalmining Communities, Nottingham, UK*, 1973.

22   Darcy Lange, *Avalanche*, p.12.

23   Willoughby Sharp, ibid., p.12.

24 *A Documentation of Bradford Working Life*, UK, 1974.

25 David Hall as quoted in Chris Meigh-Andrews, *A History of Video Art: The Development of Form and Function*, Berg, Oxford; New York, 2006, p. 7.

26 Darcy Lange, notes on the occasion of the exhibition of the works *Vern Hume* and *Clem Coxhead* at the British Film Institute, London 9 to 25 May 1975.

In an attempt to portray a cross section of the Bradford industry, Lange selected with diagrammatic care four factories – which he termed 'situations' – and in each of these, chose to record three to five workmen – which he termed 'studies'. A total of 15 studies were grouped in these four situations. Each of the 15 studies was then recorded by video takes of 10 minutes each, two takes of 16mm film (of the first and last half minute of the videotaped study), and one black and white still photograph per study. All shared the same composition, with different camera and sound techniques adapted to the rhythm of the work of each subject, alternating between hand-held camera and fixed tripod shots, and camera and location microphones.

The aim was to show activities that one normally would not see. The use of long, unedited takes gave the impression of observing, as if one was actually there. He aimed at rendering reality with the least intervention, which may explain the use of all three media, simultaneously shot and sharing the same framing, with systematic precision. His intention was to scrutinise, and represent, these work activities and to do so with a degree of objectivity. [24]

One must also note that Lange's unedited, real-time approach was due in part to the restrictions imposed by the medium itself. It might have also determined the need to structure what and how to record the subject. Limited editing facilities gave video a fairly minimal sensibility, which also coincided with the time's reductive and 'cerebral' preoccupations. [25] However, Lange's use of diagrams, as shown later for instance in his *Work Studies in Schools* series, is closer to artists, such as Steven Willats, with a strong social and political referent.

This examination of the medium's unique qualities was a dominant position of artists during the formative years of video. To some extent it mirrors and explains Lange's early reflective attention to the specificity of video in relation to the other two media. He declared: "I use video as an extension of a desire to recreate reality. This medium is appropriate because of its economy, its ability to record long takes, its mobility and its immediacy. To say that my work is entirely dependent on the nature of video is true only because of my gradual discovery and acceptance of the medium's inherent qualities and limitations". [26] In relating to the current video practice of the time, Rosetta Brooks framed Lange's work, however, outside a scene polarised

Study of an Artist at Work

by the structuralists and those taking a non-formal approach.
The former were heirs of the modernist tradition and engaged in
self-referential exercises and the exploration of medium, while the
latter (citing Bruce Nauman and Vito Acconci) were interested in
capitalising on video's 'directness' and simply recording without
any attention to the intrinsic qualities provided by the medium.[27]
Although Lange explored how we come to know things and how we
represent things, whilst occasionally engaging in the formal syntax
that could align him with some of the structuralists concerns, this
reflexivity was never the prime objective.

Lange's early interest in photographers like Dorothea Lange,
Edward Weston, Walker Evans or Lewis Hine shows his affiliation
with the possibilities of the social document and his concern to
portray his subject with a degree of respect and dignity. He said:
"We have a responsibility to keep questioning the nature and
power of realism. Are there ways for the camera to record without
stripping people of their spirit, without sloganising, without
replacing a deep sense of community by a shallow voyeurism?"[28]

Lange's *Work Studies* were not heroic, idealised depictions of
working class people. They are not personality studies, nor are the
individuals purposely anonymous. In fact, videos were often titled
after the names of those who were recorded such as in *Jack Jury,
Stockman, Urenui* (1974) or *Clem Coxhead, Study of Cow Milking
in Opunake, Taranaki* (1974). Rather, the focus seems to gravitate
towards the activity that they skilfully perform. Initially, the studies
aimed to become a document of working life in cities such as
Bradford or Birmingham. As these evolved, however, they focused
increasingly on individual working tasks, almost as studies of skill
performance, where repetition and monotony were recurrent, and
where the camera showed, literally and in real time, how these
tasks were performed. Lange defined his aims as: "My intentions
are to convey the image of work as work, as an occupation, as an
activity, as creativity and as a time consumer".[29]

A degree of referentiality appears again in these works,
systematically detailing the sequential tasks of an individual or
a group, in a factory, or over the course of the day. These were
presented in separate studies or chapters, titled after the type of task,
for instance, in *Waitara Freezing Works* (1974), with segments such
as 'Boning calves', 'Boning beef' and 'Stomach removal'. As such, the
study is almost stripped of its social or political reference and could
simply be seen as what it is: a study of labour as a performed activity.

27 Rosetta Brooks, *Studio International*,
    1973, p.109.

28 Lange, *Video Art*, p. 17.

29 Lange, Bradford Art Galleries and
    Museums, p.2.

30 *Vern Hume, Aerial Top Dressing, Taranaki*, 1974.

In the early *Work Studies*, Lange rarely spoke or interacted with his subjects in front of the camera; with exceptions such as the interview with the factory owner in *Breakers Metalworks*. The subjects were aware of the camera, in close-ups more obviously than in long shots, but most of the time they were absorbed by the tasks that occupied them. This was due also to the less pervasive nature of video at the time, when most people had never seen themselves portrayed in video before. However, in the works that he conducted in New Zealand in 1974 he often appeared in front of the camera. These videos were frequently divided into two sections: 'work', which integrated chapters depicting the variety of working tasks carried out in a day's workload or by different individuals; and 'personalisation', which included the workers' lunch break or moment of leisure. It is during these lunch break scenes that Lange appears in the footage, often sharing lunch and engaging in conversation, as seen in *Vern Hume, Aerial Top Dressing, Taranaki* (1974). [30] His subtle presence in the footage avoids attention without ignoring the level of intrusion that video recording may bring into the scene.

These interventions emphasise Lange's aim to engage with his subjects as well as recognise and document his dual position as both an outsider artist and an insider, since his New Zealand subjects were often friends and acquaintances. Lange grew up in a farming community, often helping with the tasks on the family dairy farm. In videos depicting rural labour one senses his communion with the workers portrayed and his ability to relate to them while recognising his chosen alternative position as an artist. Lange described his *Work Studies* devoted to rural labour – in Spain, Scotland and New Zealand – as a way to "go ahead to a former life". [31] By choosing to insert himself in the footage, Lange acknowledges the contingencies of objective representation, rather than adhering to strict exercises in order to achieve greater objectivity. Consequently, he provides greater transparency to his activity. Perhaps this is why in *Cantavieja, Study of Work in a Spanish Village, Spain* (1975), while living for a week among the people whom he recorded, with rudimentary Spanish, there is no lunch break scene. Every night, Lange showed them the footage taken that day. This process with his subjects would later become a common fundamental feature of his working method, incorporated into his work as in *Work Studies in Schools* (1976–7).

31 Lange, *Avalanche*, p. 13.

Study of an Artist at Work

The interaction with his subjects, something that appealed to Lange from early on, achieved further meaning in his *Work Studies in Schools* when he formalised the notion of playing his recordings back to their subjects. The first one of the series, *Study of Three Birmingham Schools, UK* (1976),[32] in many ways continued some of the concerns of the *Work Studies*. Here the activity is neither industrial, nor rural, but based around education. These are studies of teaching performances, where Lange systematically set himself to attentively record facial expressions or the use of hands or body movements in the teachers' interaction with the students, as exemplified in 'Mr. Hughes, The Wheel', a study in Leabank Junior School. The added use of video as a pedagogical tool for teachers at the School of Art Education, as Helen Legg has pointed out, was indeed an important referent in the conception of this series.[33] More importantly, Lange's studies introduced and examined language for the first time, particularly how the subject is defined by linguistic parameters marking social differences such as gender, race, class, cultural and economic backgrounds. As Lange selected private and public schools of different economic spectrums, social, as well as ideological differences now became even more apparent through language, such as in Mr. Perks's lesson on Orwell's *Animal Farm* in one of the Birmingham studies, thus, as Lange stated, aiming to "illustrate the social breakdown within each class".[34]

What distinguishes the *School Studies* series is the element of feedback, which appeared in some of the Birmingham studies but was fully developed in *Studies of Teaching in Four Oxfordshire Schools, UK* (1977).[35] For the first time, Lange played and recorded teachers teaching in the classroom, followed by the teachers' and the students' reactions to the tapes. The subjects' reactions became incorporated into the work and guided its development, and by exposing this process, Lange turned these into studies of videotaping as a work activity. As Guy Brett has argued, Lange never saw these tapes as finished works but as "researches" and "an educational process".[36] Questions were posed to his subjects regarding the validity of their representations as teachers or pupils and the accuracy of the footage and the potential function of this activity, raising expectations about the appropriate ways that the footage could be used. By doing so, Lange introduced an element of agency to the activity of video-making. By turning his subjects into their own audience, his videos radically introduced the prospect of transformation, undermining video aesthetics for

32   *Study of Three Birmingham Schools, UK*, 1976.

33   Phil Slight and Ron Jones taught at the School of Art Education. Video was used as a tool to record classes which then served as material for pedagogical analysis and discussion. Between 1971 and 1973, Lange taught at the Birmingham School of Art, of which the School of Art Education was part. This would be crucial in understanding the origins of the *Work Studies in Schools* (1976–7). Helen Legg unpublished lecture at Govett-Brewster Art Gallery, 26 August 2008.

34   Darcy Lange, *Work Studies in Schools*, Museum of Modern Art Oxford, Oxford, 1977, p. 18.

35   *Studies of Teaching in Four Oxfordshire Schools, UK*, 1977.

36   Guy Brett in his introduction to *Work Studies in Schools*, p. 3.

the potential of social change. Here is where the critique raised in relation to documentary practices comes to term as the subjects are not passively portrayed but integrate their own voices, judging and commenting on the document itself, which in turn becomes part of the document.

Video as Social Activism

When the Sony Portapak arrived, this low-cost and portable equipment was taken up by artists and community organisers wanting to produce 'television' outside the ideological and format restrictions that applied to broadcast programmes. Video activists used the medium as a tool to raise social and political consciousness, contributing to the counter-culture defined by left-wing political agendas. In the UK, radical video groups looked upon electronic media as a reaction to broadcast television. The Portapak was often described as "the basic means of the individual decentralisation of TV technology", where "decentralisation, flexibility, immediacy of playback" were keystones. [37]

As Lange's interests evolved beyond merely recording the social reality of working life, the immediacy of the medium became a determinant for the communicative aspirations he sought for his work. It allowed him to show his videotapes to the subjects he portrayed, and through this engagement with his subjects, he saw the potential to effect change. By 1975, Lange defined his work as "being something very close to social activism", and expressed the need to be more inclusive and to reach out to larger audiences, "this is where I need to get a lot more serious about getting the work shown to a wider audience, and making a real effort to get back to the people it was recorded from". [38] As far back as 1974, Lange looked forward to presenting the material recorded to the workers of his Bradford factory series, but the opening of the show would be delayed four years, presumably because of the controversial nature of the material. [39]

Lange, like most of his contemporary video artists, had no overt aspirations regarding the commercial art gallery scene. On the contrary, he sought for his work to reach a wider audience and a place in the broader cultural context. Aware he was perceived as an outsider and of the difficulties of relating sometimes to the people portrayed, even validating his activity as work, Lange felt the need to transgress the boundaries of the art world: "... why should a videographer be confined to galleries and the art

37 John Hopkins and Sue Hall 'The Metasoftware of Video' in *Studio International*, May/June 1976, p. 260.

38 Lange, *Avalanche*, p. 13.

39 Lange, *Video Art*, p. 9.

world?"[40] Subscribing to the Marxist ideology common among video practitioners of the time, Lange shared the ideals of the democratisation of culture conveyed by Mao Tse-Tung: "Why should art be the domain of the few and not the many? Shouldn't democratisation of culture, and, in our case, of liberation of communications technology for public access, be an integral part of our actual art activity? We demand the unity of technology, art and politics; the unity of information, meaning and effect".[41] However, for Lange the potential power of video to liberate extended beyond the democratisation of culture and issues of information access. His belief had to do with the immediate communicative relation with his subjects – and thus its potential to effect change in them, one which he saw as reciprocal.

As Guy Brett indicates, Lange's work must be framed in the context of a decade of intense politicisation in the UK that found its parallel in New Zealand's political climate. In New Zealand, this coincided with a period known as the Māori Renaissance, which centred around the revision of Māori land rights. A moment that crystallised with Bastion Point in 1977–8,[42] was one of the most public incidents of New Zealand's history, it contested the government's right to take over Māori land. In 1977, Lange joined with the activist impulses and activities of other fellow documentary film-makers and photographers, sharing their aims to use their tools to help raise awareness and support for the retaining and returning of land to the Māori people. These recordings became the *Māori Land Project* (1977–80) and concentrate mostly on two cases: Bastion Point and the Ngātihine Block, north of Auckland. The former represented a struggle centring on confiscated land that triggered confrontation with the government and police, and resulted in the incarceration of those who refused to leave the site. The latter was a legal battle to retain land from being leased by a forestry corporation under the premise that is was poorly administrated and underdeveloped by the Māori owners.

However, unlike journalistic approaches that concentrated on the news stories of the Bastion Point gathering at the crucial moment of bulldozing the last building on the marae, where the Hawkes family had held fast for 508 days to resist occupation, Lange's account was far more invested, personalised and intimate, as he followed the family's daily lives over these months, spending time with them on the marae, thereby portraying them in their home environment. As he became more involved in the Māori

40 Ibid., p. 7.

41 As quoted in John Hopkins and Sue Hall, 'The Metasoftware of Video' in *Studio International*, May/June 1976, p. 260. This important issue devoted entirely to video includes articles offering the current state of video in different countries and with a focus on specific artists. Lange is featured in this issue with a monographic article.

42 *Māori Land Project*, 1977–80.

political cause, he grew ever more committed to video's power and efficacy as a tool for political action and educational purposes.

In 1979, after numerous trips from London, Lange finally relocated to the Netherlands to teach at the Academy of Art and Design (AKI) in Enschede. It was in the Netherlands where he further developed the ideas and aspirations of the *Māori Land Project*. In Amsterdam he began working with René Coelho, founder of the new Montevideo/Time Based Arts, with whom he produced a programme for NOS Television based on the *Māori Land Project*. In Utrecht, he met Leonard Henny, professor at the Sociological Institute's Centre for International Development Education, and with him produced *The Māori Land Struggle*, which focused on Bastion Point. The result of these collaborations – a 30 minute television documentary, a three-part sociological analysis made with Utrecht University, and a documentary by Lange – were shown in *The Land of the Māori* exhibition at the Van Abbemuseum in Eindhoven and the Internationaal Cultureel Centrum in Antwerp, Belgium in 1980. This project marks a politically conscious shift towards a collaborative practice and was influenced by Māori ideas about collectivism.

It is through Lange's collaborations with Henny and the Victor Hara Collective, during the development of this exhibition in 1979, that the notion of media manipulation and the political structures exercised by television became his focus. Here, using Lange's footage of Bastion Point, different versions were edited for different purposes: for three different publics (television audiences, students, and museum visitors); by three different agents (a television producer, a sociologist, and an artist), and three different institutions (broadcast organisation, university, and museum). It is easy to see this project, with its various components, as a continuation of his interest in 'objectivity' and 'truth' which motivated his early use of different media. Now the focus had been transferred from the material and formal constituencies of the different representational media to issues relating to montage, the plurality of publics and theoretical frameworks that shaped the form and content of this work. It was meant as an experiment in media analysis exposing the influential, or manipulative, power of media, and how form and content were determined by the intended target audience.

The segment that Lange produced for this exhibition included video and film, experimenting with editing and sound techniques (using, for example, Eisenstein's silent narrative style). Decisions were driven by a desire to produce a "documentary quality of scientific research", where accuracy proved pivotal in an "attempt to provide legal proof". By way of example, Lange used the material chronologically and chose film and video to give "a more truthful documentary value – by the contrasting media", as was the case in his early *Work Studies*. His videotape footage accounted for a total of 30 hours conducted over the course of three trips to New Zealand between 1977 and 1980. [43]

In an attempt to raise international awareness about the Māori political situation, Lange took part in the Fourth Russell Tribunal in Rotterdam in 1980. With the help of Henny, Lange was instrumental in securing the participation of representatives of South Pacific indigenous groups, even though the conference focused on North American and South American indigenous issues. He videotaped the event, which is part of the *Māori Land Project*, including interventions by an Aboriginal Australian, an Eskimo from Greenland, Myron Mataoa from Tahiti representing Polynesia, and Colin Clark, a spokesman for the Māori people in Aotearoa, New Zealand.

In the spirit of the *Māori Land Project* and of this growing political commitment, Lange embarked on a new project in the Netherlands, *People of the World* (1983), [44] this time involving his music as flamenco guitarist. [45] This project was clearly influenced by Henny's audiovisual productions aimed at raising awareness of the responsibilities of the Dutch population to the problems faced by 'Third World' communities living in the Netherlands. Lange conceived this multimedia opera in collaboration with René van Hoften, and it premiered at the RASA Cultural Centre in Utrecht on 16 and 17 June, 1983. The event looked at music as a channel for bringing together the cultures of the immigrant communities living in the Netherlands, in Lange's words: "a kind of musical meetinghouse". [46] Thirty-five musicians from seven countries – The Netherlands, Spain, Morocco, Turkey, the Maluku Islands, Suriname, and Greece – performed in front of huge projections of a selection of images from Lange's previous works. Lange was credited as freelance director and spiritual father of this production and performed flamenco guitar. The project employed traditional folk music as a means to escape the alienation of the immigrant condition and lessen the discrimination to which these groups were subjected. When Lange relocated to New Zealand

43   Lange, *Darcy Lange Māori Land Project*, Stedelijk Van Abbemuseum, Eindhoven, and Internationaal Cultureel Centrum, Antwerp, 1980, pp. 34–5.

44   Darcy Lange and Maria Snijders performing flamenco guitar in *People of the World*, 1983–4.

45   Lange dedication to the flamenco music in Spain came about also through Phil Slight. Slight, a flamenco guitarist and flamencologist, introduced Lange to Don Pohren, an American flamencologist and author of several books on the subject, who had written on the maestro of flamenco guitar, Diego del Gastor, from Morón de la Frontera (Seville, Spain). Lange subsequently studied with Gastor in Morón in the summers from 1969 until Gastor's death in 1973. Bob Ellis, in phone conversation with the author, 29 September 2008.

His commitment to flamenco guitar continued throughout his life.In the *Māori Land Project* catalogue Lange pays tribute to Gastor, he wrote: "I would like to dedicate my contribution of the exhibition to the memory, depth, warmth and creativity of the man and his music, the gypsy flamenco guitarist Diego del Gastor". Lange, ibid., p. 41.

For further detail, see Pedro G. Romero's *Antipodes: Darcy Lange, Work and Flamenco in the Image Chain of Production* in this publication.

46   Lange, *Video Art*, p. 88.

in early 1984, the project was handed over to the Kultureel Front in Utrecht, which then managed its tour to theatres around the country. It eventually became a special UNESCO performance. Lange's correspondence indicates discussions about the making of a 5 ½ hour television series, each chapter devoted to specific cultures and workers, and a book of texts relating the experiences of these immigrant communities living in the Netherlands, which never materialised for reasons unknown. [47]

Following the steps of *People of the World* in an attempt to fuse his music and video practice, Lange created the "ecological media opera" *Aire del Mar* (1988), [48] which he performed with his wife Maria Snijders and other participants, such as the New Zealand poet Denys Trussell reading the poetry of Federico García Lorca. This multimedia performance featured live music, with video and slide projections providing an audiovisual backdrop. Lange played flamenco guitar, Snijders sang Spanish songs, danced, clapped and played castanets, and also directed the choreography. Projected on three screens, the slides presented an array of images celebrating nature, music and peace: landscapes from Aotearoa New Zealand, and Andalusia, flamenco and fiestas, Goya's paintings and lithographs from *The Disasters of War*, and photographs and video stills of Lange's earlier *Work Studies* series. Two monitors placed between the screens showed a selection of Lange's videos, such as the *Cantavieja* or *Bradford Working Life* series, characterising the industrial and rural realities of work, thus adding an additional aural layer to the live music. Midway through the performance, live music gave way to a video addressing the nuclear testing conducted in the South Pacific by the French Government during the early 1960s, and the environmental, political and social effects that this had on the nations of Polynesia (prompting a rapid process of independence). The 1985 South Pacific Forum had recently ended in Rarotonga with the signing of the Nuclear Free Zone agreement. The performance's message: ecological (joining the anti-nuclear global perspective), pacifist and multicultural (embracing the indigenous cultures and in favour of Māori land rights) are summarised by Lange with these words: "the underlying essence will be Land-Peace-People". [49] Ultimately, the work merges Andalusian gypsy and Māori ancestral spiritual beliefs. *Aire del Mar* was performed throughout the country in public art galleries and theatres from 1988 until 1994.

47 A letter gives indications of the difficulties that the Kultureel Front faced with managing *People of the World* as they were in need of financial support to tour the project. Unpublished letter from Richard Tuhumuri to the artist, dated 8 October 1982. Courtesy of the Darcy Lange Archive, Govett-Brewster Art Gallery.

48 Darcy Lange and Maria Snijders performing *Aire del Mar*, 1988.

49 Darcy Lange's proposal of *Aire del Mar – Hau Moana Ocean Wind*. Unpublished letter to Wellington City Art Gallery dated 16 October 1987. Courtesy of the Darcy Lange archive at the Govett-Brewster Art Gallery.

In referring to *Aire del Mar*, Lange expressed his growing interest in music as his main artistic expression. He wrote, "this programme reflects my long-planned hope of moving away from video into a marriage between my musical worlds and the forming of these audio-visual, live music, ethnographic and musical creations out of a range of music and dance". [50] Lange retired from video activity for over a decade, devoting himself almost exclusively to flamenco music. In his later years, however, he produced what became his last works, *Artist, Musicians and Poets at Work* (1999–2000), a series of documentary portraits of New Zealand's leading figures, intended as a document of historical significance. With these portraits Lange sought to present a kind of counter-television, following the steps of his early 'real-time', sparse-editing approach. The series was aired on the independent Triangle Television channel in Auckland.

Unlike that of other practitioners, Lange's affiliation with the social documentary tradition does not fall within the theoretical approaches of his contemporaries, such as Victor Burgin, Martha Rosler or Allan Sekula. Even though these artists might have been on his radar, Lange's practice clearly stands at a distance. Despite Lange's objective of constructing alternative frameworks and procedures for video, his approach lacks the critical formulation of such artists and theoreticians. One reason may be attributed to video's incipient history when compared with photography or film. For it is only in the last decade that video's own historicity has emerged as a thematic subject. While the 1970s brought the beginning of historical and theoretical reformulations in photographic practices, this decade marked the very origins of video. It was during this time that video artists like Lange were exploring the medium without the theoretical and historical framework available today. The dearth of theoretical writing at the time meant that the new medium would be framed within other histories – whether modernist, coming out of the visual arts, or around television – leaving many singular practitioners outside these discourses. More than social commentary, Lange's videos leave a trace of historical relevance, as they are documents of working people who would have otherwise remained invisible. Furthermore, the power of Lange's video-making lies in its agency – with its subjects being both portrayed and serving as active audience and participant – which imbues Lange's work with its most relevant political dimension.

50 Ibid.

Works, 1971–3

Irish Roadworkers, 1971
Installation at Royal College
of Art, London

Social Consideration, Communication and Observation, 1971

← A hardware store employee in South Kensington, London.
↑ A woman putting out her washing in London.

35

Studies of Family Groups, 1972

↑   Basil Cox in Maida Vale, London
→   Mr. and Mrs. Mates and family in Kent
     House, Pimlico, London

*Five Working Studies in British Factories
and Workplaces, UK*, 1972

Breakers Metalworks, Balsall Heath,
Birmingham.

Five Working Studies in British Factories
and Workplaces, UK, 1972

E. Brennan General Woodcarving
Furniture Workshop, London.

*Five Working Studies in British Factories
and Workplaces, UK*, 1972

Marbett Manufacturing Co. Ltd.,
London.

*Five Working Studies in British Factories
and Workplaces, UK*, 1972

Burns and Lux, London.

44

*Five Working Studies in British Factories
and Workplaces, UK*, 1972

Wild, Mellor and Bromley, Leicester.

Darcy Lange: Paco Campana[1]

Benjamin H. D. Buchloh

> We have a responsibility to keep questioning the nature and
> power of realism. Are there ways for the camera to record
> without stripping people of their spirit, without sloganising,
> without replacing a deep sense of community by a shallow
> voyeurism? My video work has always been an engagement
> with questions of this kind.
>
> Darcy Lange [2]

Ever since Robert Rauschenberg's first photographic image
collections had been recognised as an inevitable episteme of the
aesthetic of the 20th century, image accumulations by artists
from Andy Warhol to Gerhard Richter had been historically
motivated by their focus on the regime of the photographic itself.
It had become increasingly impossible to ignore the collective
pervasiveness of those images in the construction of the visual
field and the subject's perception. But neither Rauschenberg's, nor
Warhol's, and least of all the photographic accumulations of the
conceptualist artists, had been driven by the desire for a consistent
iconography. They had been engaged in neither a topical
narrativity, nor the documentation of particular historical, social or
political conditions that had been previously defined as the realm
of the photographic document.

It is thus not accidental at all that the consideration
of documentary photography re-emerges as a historical and
theoretical problem at the moment of the mid-1970s, at the apex,
so to speak, of the anti-photographic practices of conceptual
art. These critiques of conceptualist photography were primarily
voiced by a group of artists who themselves would soon emerge
as some of the key theoreticians of photographic history, or as
the practitioners of new photographic approaches to public
social life: Victor Burgin in England, Jeff Wall in Canada, and
Fred Lonidier, Martha Rosler, Allan Sekula, living and working
in California at the time (as though the pervasive presence of the
modernist dogma in New York had prohibited any reflection on
modernism's repressed photographic subtexts). And these new
critiques and historical recoveries were also formulated, quite

1   Paco Campana was one of Darcy
    Lange's artistic names as flamenco
    guitarist. In Europe, Lange would
    also perform as Paco de Taranaki
    (Taranaki being his region, as often
    flamenco artistic names include their
    town or region of origin). It was later,
    in returning to New Zealand, when
    he changed his artistic name to Paco
    Campana. By 'Campana' ('bell' in
    Spanish) Lange, whose Spanish was
    restricted, meant 'campaña' (plain) as
    in 'campo' (country).

2   Darcy Lange, *Video Art*, The
    Department of Film, Television and
    Media Studies, University of Auckland,
    Auckland, 2001, p. 17.

independently, with uncommon programmatic clarity in the work of the New Zealand artist Darcy Lange who had studied sculpture in London at the Royal College of Art from 1968 to 1971.

In 2001, in an autobiographical reflection on the development of his work, he stated: "Period One is the end of my Sculpture Period at the Royal College of Art and with that a movement into the document area of film and photography, especially the photography of Dorothea Lange, Edward Weston, Walker Evans and others."[3]

I recognise – and want to emphasise immediately – that this generation of post-conceptualist photographers had been a very diverse group of artists/authors indeed. Yet it should also be understood that they shared not only an interest in the history of documentary photography and its recovery, but also the historical urgency with which they wanted to re-define questions of photographic theory and artistic practice in opposition to the massive deskilling and de-historisation that photography had suffered at the hands of the Pop artists and the conceptualists' assault on the referentiality and historicity of photography.

Nevertheless, the motivations of that generation of artists to critique the anti-photographic photography of the conceptualists were in many ways divided, if not incompatible (one only has to think of the manifest differences between the work of Allan Sekula and Jeff Wall). Yet all of these artists initiated various projects of the recovery of the documentary dimension of photography and its traditions, the recovery of the photographic referent, and of narrative, in short, the recovery of all of the social and political functions that documentary photography had once presumably performed. Most of the artists engaged in this project, however, understood from the start that this recovery project would inevitably imply a self-critical reflection on the legacies of documentary photography. In order to reconstruct this historical opposition, I will have to recollect, however rapidly, the key concerns that had motivated the photography of conceptualist anti-photography. These were manifold, of course, and I will only single out the most prominent ones, those that would be at the centre of the critiques of the following generation.

1. Deskilling Photography

The first topic had been the conceptualist photographers' abolition of photographic skills: Ed Ruscha, Dan Graham, Douglas

3   Ibid., p. 18.

Darcy Lange: Paco Campana

Huebler, John Baldessari, Robert Smithson, to name only the most prominent ones, had programmatically assaulted photographic techniques as an art or as a craft. These conventions of artisanal and technological production that had defined photography since its inception were systematically and ostentatiously discarded or wilfully ignored (the grand exception to this agenda was of course the work of Bernd and Hilla Becher, who – while clearly integral participants of the rise of conceptualist photographic practices – insisted from the very beginning on the continuation, or rather, the resurrection of the skills of the German photographic traditions of Weimar Neue Sachlichkeit).

2. Anti-Narrative Photography

The conceptualists' post-Duchampian approach in fact treated the photographic image as a ready-made (as Ed Ruscha repeatedly stated), which was of course the very epistemic model from which the arsenal of deskilling strategies had been initially drawn. Yet conceptualist photography drew equally on what we could call the neo-positivist project of deconstructing narrativity that had been at the centre of the nouveau roman since the 1950s. Dan Graham, for one, had frequently argued that Michel Butor and Alain Robbe-Grillet had been key references for the development of his artistic operations. Their defiance of representational writing, and their critique of the historical credibility of narrative structures, were among the primary reasons for his attraction to the *nouveau roman*.

3. Anti-Authorial Photography

Both the Duchampian ready-made and the *nouveau roman* model had held one additional prophecy at the beginning of the 1960s: authorial anonymity, or – as it had been famously identified in Roland Barthes's prognosis – 'The Death of the Author'. It is certainly more than serendipitous that this essay had been first commissioned and published in English by one of the key figures in post-minimal and conceptual criticism, the artist Brian O'Doherty when he edited a special issue of *Aspen* magazine in 1967 which published work by Dan Graham side by side with work by Robbe-Grillet and Duchamp. Thus the post-minimalist and conceptual artists defined photography from the start as a set of ideal tools for the project of de-authorisation and de-subjectivisation: it was mechanical, widely distributed, a common cultural and industrial device that was collectively available and practised in myriad amateurish applications. Furthermore, it supposedly liberated both author and spectator from reading conventions tied to the privileges of an educated audience.

Typically, Lange in his conversation with Willoughby Sharp stated later: "this is where I need to get a lot more serious about getting the work shown to a wider audience, and making a real effort to get back to the people it was recorded from", and speaks of his practice as "social activism". [4]

In short, photography promised the perfect fusion of some of the fundamental concerns of the conceptualists: to negate conventional forms of subject formation, and to contest the cultural constitution of the subject in privileged forms of experience altogether. Instead, conceptual photography aimed to confront the actually governing conditions of the photographic image regimes that controlled the everyday life of the masses contained within the industrial apparatus of advertisement and consumption.

4. Anti-Pictorial Photography

It is against this extreme ambiguity between the painterly, the structural and the photographic as it had been initially introduced by painters such as Rauschenberg, Richter and Warhol, that Dan Graham's photographic work of mid-1960 in particular, staged an initial reclamation of the hidden referential, and iconic dimensions of the documentary photography. Graham invoked – perhaps before anybody else – the legacies of Walker Evans, initiating the recovery of some of the traditional functions of photography, the image's referential powers, the factual and the documentary dimensions, and transferring them into the artistic discussions after conceptualism.

5. Archive Aesthetics

One could argue furthermore that one of the additional effects of the 'death of the artistic author' and of a general project of de-subjectivisation, was not necessarily – or not exclusively – as Barthes's prognosis had suggested, the 'birth of the reader,' but it had also become a contributory cause to the rise of an aesthetic of the archive. Therefore it is not surprising that anonymity and anomie became the principle of the conceptualist's archive without historical agency and aspirations.

The systematic exploration of photographic image regimes, embodied in archival structures and aleatory collections that were

4   Ibid., p. 18.

not necessarily guided by any evident principles of motivated photographic signs or coherent iconographies, but rather by the seemingly wilful randomness of the universal permeation of the everyday by these image regimes, became the determining episteme of photographic activities within the context of conceptual photography.

Obvious examples would be Ed Ruscha's photographic books, Dan Graham's photographic collections, Douglas Huebler's image collections of a large and random set of photographic records tracing both acts of temporal and spatial expansiveness, Gerhard Richter's *Atlas*, Robert Smithson's accumulated photographs (and, once again, a manifest counter-example would be of course what we would have to call the motivated archive, the work of the Bechers, even though their project still shares the condition of interminability and a sheer infinite expansive accumulation).

Potentially interminable in temporal or spatial extension, these archival collections become a fundamental organising principle for the infinity of random, expandable quantities of image equivalents. It was in these archives that the principle of systematic deskilling and the principle of the universal equivalence of all iconic source material came together and found their historical articulation.

The programmatic absence of agency and the elision of authorial determination were thus common to all of these operations. In fact, precisely these absences made up the radicality of these artistic practices, imbuing them with a momentary critical potential. In the same manner that the ready-made and the *nouveau roman* had excelled at suddenly confronting spectatorial or readerly expectations with a heretofore unimaginable freedom of unguided and uncontrolled experiences of the involuntarily operative principles of linguistic or iconic systems of the everyday, the critique and subversion inherent in these photographic practices negated any previously held principle of authorial motivation, of organisation, or any systematic execution and production.

Lange identified the 'archival impulse' early on as an inevitable and desirable side effect of the new technologies of video recording, explicitly singling out video's archival functions. Yet it is also instantly evident that his conception of an archive differs fundamentally from the archival impulses of the conceptualist photographers:

(Video) has the value of sound tape but only with pictures. It is a great imitating medium. It is good for archiving folklore. It is good for replacing bad television. It is probably going to replace many a library book. It is essentially an archival medium and that is something that the commercial side has not yet grasped. [5]

6. The Social Document

Thus the recovery of the photographic image for artistic production of the 1960s in general, and the usages of photographic imagery in the practices of Pop Art and conceptualism in particular, had obliterated a broad range of particular photographic traditions. The focus on deskilling, the insistent demands for radical de-authorisation, the seemingly subversive insistence on iconic demotivation, and the cynical or indifferent construction of an involuntary and decentred archive, all of these strategies had systematically obscured whole histories and epistemic formations that previously had been foundational to photographic meaning.

What had been disavowed most of all was of course the definition of the photograph as a document, or more precisely as a social document; as an image that gave a relatively reliable account of structures, processes, performances, contexts, determinations, and, most importantly of all, of agency, both on the side of the photographic author, as much as on the side of the photographed subjects and communities.

In whatever ways we would want to define the photographic document, a most elementary definition would have to include the following: that it presumes agency (both on the side of the author as much as on the side of the depicted subjects and communities), that it presumes the possibility of a motivation of the signifying process, that it assumes the implied dimensions of communicative action in the photographic representation, and that it aims at the cohesive organisation of a narrative in both individual images and their archival accumulation as a desirable and available structure. It also presumes, most importantly perhaps, the desire for either a mnemonic retrieval of political critique or a horizon of social transformation, an intervention within the merely given facticity of everyday life.

Some of the most important examples of this definition of the documentary photograph in the 20th century would be of course the very figures already mentioned, the photographers that Darcy Lange and the post-conceptualist generation would now

5   Lange, op. cit., p. 12.

rediscover, be it the work of Lewis Hine, or the practices of the American project of the FSA photographers of the 1930s such as Ben Shahn, Dorothea Lange and Walker Evans. They would, however, reconsider these figures not only in terms of a forgotten photographic history, but more importantly in terms of their aesthetic legacies.[6] But what I stated initially should be repeated: that it is that very same generation of artists already mentioned, i.e. Burgin, Lonidier, Rosler, and Sekula in particular, who at that moment begin to explicitly respond in both their works and their writings to the perceived limitations of the conceptualist legacies. Fred Lonidier's *29 Arrests* (1972) – made as an explicit critical rebuttal of Ed Ruscha's works – would be one example; Allan Sekula's *Untitled Slide Sequence* (1972), of workers leaving the General Dynamics Convair Division Aerospace Corporation's manufacturing site in San Diego would be another; and Martha Rosler's photographic project *The Bowery in Two Inadequate Descriptive Systems* (1974) would be a third. These artistic projects of the early to mid-1970s were accompanied, of course, by the first major essays of that generation, notably Sekula's 'Dismantling Modernism, Re-inventing Documentary', and Rosler's 'In, Around and Afterthoughts on Documentary Photography' published in 1978 and 1981 respectively. But none of these authors advocated merely a simplistic return to the tradition of documentary photography as an answer to the major epistemological problem that the apparent defeat and prohibition of referentiality and representation had posed for politically conscious and historically committed writers and artists. Rather, all of them took their investigation of the historical repression and disavowal of the documentary practices as much as documentary's increasingly obvious insufficiencies and failures, both in the past and in the present, as the stepping stones for a new theorisation and representational practice of the socio-political referent in photography.

Inevitably – or so it seems at least with historical hindsight – did the search for predecessors and antecedents, lead to yet another obscured history of the 20th century, one which would also encounter rediscovery and reconsideration for the first time during those years: the legacies of Soviet factography and the Weimar workers' photography clubs.

And if scholarly inspiration and the desire for paradigm shifts in what appeared to be the limitations of the present, might have legitimised these changes by re-discovering previously established and then forgotten or repressed practices,

6   It should be noted, perhaps, that by the early to mid-1970s, the history of FSA photography had not yet become a universally discussed subject of photographic history writing, not even by the historians of the medium itself. Allan Trachtenberg's breakthrough study of American photographs from Matthew Brady to Walker Evans, for example, was not published until 1989.

these changes also encountered immediately prejudicial condemnations. Traditionalist art historians and critics, and most obviously, the stubborn disinterest of the institutionally and commercially organised segments of cultural production, made those resistances as substantial as possible. Most common was the strategy to falsely establish a connection between concepts of photographic documentary and the highly discredited legacies of what was universally derided as 'socialist realism'. Here is an example of a review by Michael Brenson, written for *The New York Times* in 1984, in response to an exhibition segment of work by Allan Sekula and Fred Lonidier that I had curated at the New Museum in New York that year:

> Fred Lonidier and Allan Sekula were invited (to the exhibition) by Benjamin H. D. Buchloh. On the whole, the work has the earnestness, conviction, and literal base of Socialist Realism. It would be hard to find work more propagandistic than Fred Lonidier's 'L.A. Public Workers Point to Some Problems: Sketches of the Present, Point to the Future for All?' which consists of photographs and tracts on subjects like 'Crises of Western Capital,' which the artist has intended for labor-union walls.

And indeed, Brenson got one thing right, that is, the renewed quest for 'realism'. But the critic's modernist blindness had compelled him to associate realism with the most unrealistic of all artistic practices, the so-called 'socialist realist painting'. The term, by which this erasure had been most successfully accomplished, was the most powerfully suggestive discreditation of any kind of representation, namely that of 'propaganda' and it too was inevitably deployed in Brenson's statement.

Darcy Lange would knowingly adopt the very term of 'social realism' with hindsight, yet inverting it into the heretofore-unknown concept of what he calls "uncomplimentary" when describing the development of his work studies projects:

> Then I realised that I had an impossible task of trying to select a cross section of work and people; so gradually, as I worked I progressed into video style and instead of selecting groups of people I narrowed it down to one person for each job ... With the tightening of the video camera style and with the

observation centred around that one person, various qualities came forward. The studies became performance analysis, they searched the monotony of the work, they questioned the work load [sic] and the suffering due to the work, and they became a kind of uncomplimentary social realism. [7]

'Propaganda' had been (and continues to be) the key concept with which the Western capitalist world – in particular since the decades of the Cold War – had successfully contained its own condition of being the most propagandistic society human history has ever known (is there an artistic practice that could be more propagandistic than that of Jeff Koons or Damien Hirst?).

Throughout the first three decades after the war, 'propaganda' had been deployed to discredit any type of documentary, let alone politically progressive and activist work, whether it would be that of the 1920s in Weimar Germany, or that of the Soviet Union. Regardless of whether it had been the factographic photography of Alice Lex Nerlinger in Berlin, or that of the Soviet factographers, or whether it had been the complex narrative realism in the radical re-definitions of photomontage practices in the hands of John Heartfield or Josep Renau, all had been written out of the history of modernism throughout the 1970s under the discrediting auspices of 'propaganda'. The term would be inevitably deployed again when the younger generation of post-conceptualist artists reconsidered the legacies of documentary photography.

What was at stake, then, for that generation of artists and writers was to find a set of strategies and artistic and discursive operations that would allow reconsidering a socio-historical aesthetic of representation and referentiality. Furthermore, it would have to be a photographic or a filmic aesthetic that would not only be fully aware of the historical failures and insufficiencies of earlier practices of committed documentary. It would, at the same time, have to find ways to revise and re-engage all of these legacies and incorporate them into the present, within an explicitly anti-conceptual and anti-structuralist aesthetic project, and also recognise the advances of more commonly available media technology such as video that had appeared since the early 1960s.

The Working Body, Sculpture and its Representation
With the rediscovery of these factographic practices and of the collectivist organisations of the worker's photography

7   Lange, op. cit., pp. 43–4.

Benjamin H. D. Buchloh

clubs of Weimar Germany and the Soviet Union, came also the reconsideration of one of the most, if not the deepest prohibition, in modernist culture: the representation of the working body, and the representation of the social classes performing the invisible and un-representable acts of physical labour, the class in fact, that had once been called the 'working class'. Obviously, I cannot even begin to elaborate the complex arguments with which this prohibition of the labouring body had been initiated and had become one of the silent and enduring doxas in the field of modernist representation.

Yet I should also state immediately that this interdiction to represent labour had originated in some of the convictions most fundamental and essential to modernism's progressive promises: after all, modernist culture wanted to be the culture of a symbolic critique of alienation, a culture of a subversive resistance against universal instrumentalisation by calling upon the subject's ludic imaginary. In order to perform these oppositions in public, it had to act as a culture of negating labour and refuse any participation in the false heroicisation of work. Most importantly, it had to resist any celebratory affirmation of the oppressed labouring body in representation, since such a representation could only have served as a function and site of legitimatisation for precisely those forms of subjection and alienation that modernism had set out to oppose most vociferously from the start.

This prohibition on images of labour had in fact served as one of the most integral definitions of what cultural representation would have to achieve: it had to perform the ludic negation of necessity, and it had to induce the semblance of the subject's universal access to acts of self-determination and self-constitution outside of the realm of instrumentalisation. And, by contrast, whenever the labouring body did find a representation in the 20th century – apart from the already mentioned photographic and factographic practices – it had instantly turned into the most deceptive and oppressive idealisation of the deepest forms of alienated labour, as in the representations of the worker in the images of state socialism and the idolisations of physical labour in images of the fascist ideologies.

The recovery of the working body in post-conceptual art thus necessitated a very complex set of diverse operations, performed, as I would argue, at the beginning of the 1970s, in Lange's astonishing photography and video work. The first operation was of course to comprehend the necessity for sculptural production itself to assume again a manifest relationship to the material and physiological processes of material and temporal transformation. It required further to recognise that these processes inevitably would have to situate sculpture within the very technologies of surveillance and recording temporality that had become the industry standards by the end of the 1960s. This, obviously, placed Lange – along with his friend and early supporter, Dan Graham, [8] – in manifest opposition to the culmination of the concealment of labour and production in the minimalist practices of the 1960s. Minimalism, as is well known – with very few exceptions like Robert Morris – had celebrated precisely the invisibility of actual production and the anonymity of labour as one of its most provocative achievements.

But Lange does not only re-incorporate the somatic dimension of production and the performative dimensions of sculptural execution into the recording of spatio-temporal processes of the situated body in space. Bruce Nauman and Dan Graham had positioned themselves most polemically against the minimalists through this manifest and literal 'incorporation' of both the making and the viewing processes, leading to a phenomenological radicalisation. While clearly indebted to their definitions of the sculptural body as a performing body, Lange reversed their stances dialectically by situating the principle of sculptural production now in the very performative operations of labour and production at large as they occur at all times within the bodies of the labouring collective. [9] So what had been the necessary, yet empty, bodily phenomenological exercises and task performances, for example in Bruce Nauman's acting in the studio in 1968, now became the full and functional performances of the school teacher teaching a class of students, or the farm labourer scything or ploughing the earth in Spain. In a statement on a videotape of the daily labour of sheep farmers in Scotland, Lange makes an exceptionally explicit remark about his efforts to distance his work from that of the photography and sculpture of his conceptualist and post-minimalist predecessors:

> It ended up as a video portrait of a day's work by four
> shepherds in Dumfrieshire, Scotland. In some ways
> the videotape was a satire of a Richard Long walk that I
> had seen on film, and I must say it was and perhaps is

8   Lange recalled in 2001: "I met Dan Graham first on return from the 1974–1975 visit to New Zealand ... Dan was extremely friendly and immediately offered me a place to stay. It was as though we had known each other for a year, marking the beginning of a friendship which today is still intact. Dan is one of the few artists who is constantly looking at other art than his own, and has consistently tried and successfully helped many artists to get established." Ibid., p. 78.

9   *Competition Axemen at Agricultural and Pastoral Show, Stratford, Taranaki,* 1974.

one of the truest balances between conceptual art and a documentation of actual work or social reality. [10]

Ranging from steelworkers to schoolteachers in England, from farm labourers and musicians performing in Lange's beloved second country, Spain, to the sheep-shearing Māori of his home in New Zealand, Lange started to build an archive of video recordings of labour and production. His unedited and uncut real time recordings of these processes achieve, in fact, precisely the realism in the depiction of labour that had been absent from almost all representations since the 1920s (with the exception of the factographic photographs of the workers' photography clubs in Weimar and in the Soviet Union, and the films of Robert Flaherty or the Dutch Joris Ivens from the same period). What is most important, perhaps, are the implications in Lange's epistemological reversals of the video documentary for the issues sketched out in the first part of the essay: first of all, with regard to the question of deskilling.

What is defined by Lange is not just a critique of the dead end of the once historically radical project of deskilling in the hands of an ever expanding culture industry production of deskilled objects laying claim to be works of art, a deluge whose consequences we are now witnessing everywhere in heretofore unimaginable quantities. Neither is he advocating a reactionary return to a mythical principle of artistic skills, as it had been re-enacted by many painters at precisely that moment of post-conceptual aesthetics.

In fact, Lange was arguing from the start for a dramatically different third position, one that recognises the universal permeation and presence of skills in every member of the working collectivity. Furthermore, he recognises the performance of these artisan, technical, pedagogical skills as the foundation of a socially unrecognised subjectivity (in contrast to the hypertrophic cult of the artist for example), an authorial presence that surpasses by far the mere claim, or assignment to an admittedly once radical promise to transform authors into readers.

Lange's persistent interest in the conditions of social class would almost guarantee the failure of the reception of his work beyond the narrowest group of friends and allies over the years. [11] It would also eventually appear as an epistemological fallacy, separating Lange's work almost irreconcilably from that of his friend and in many ways influential peer, Dan Graham. After

10 Ibid., p. 37.

11 As already mentioned, one of Lange's most loyal supporters was – and remains – Dan Graham. By the mid-1970s Jack Wendler, a key dealer in the history of international conceptual art, and co-founder with Peter Townsend of *Art Monthly*, supported Lange for a while, exhibiting his work in 1973, as did David Elliott, then director of the Museum of Modern Art Oxford, in 1977.

Darcy Lange: Paco Campana

all, Graham's work remained deeply attached to a structuralist and post-structuralist critique of the traditional forms of subject formation, a critique that necessitated the abolition of the concept of agency and authorial identity.

For Lange, by contrast and in programmatic opposition to the work of the post-minimalists, the agency and the authorial initiative of the anonymously labouring subject would be central to his construction of a dialectical model of subject formation. After all, it has become evident over the recent past with the urgency of an imminent catastrophe, that it is only in the recognition of the subject's skills and capacities to produce and reproduce itself in acts of work and production, that the subject can constitute itself and resist a final and fatal process of collective de-sublimation. In fact, in view of the total devastation of subjectivity that the culture of consumption has wrought onto the collectivity, it appears as though the sole remaining forms of economic, political and psychological resistance and opposition can be found in the subject's foundation in gestures and practices of skilled forms of knowledge and production.

But Lange's schismatic wandering between New Zealand, England and Spain, and the splitting of his artistic identity between being the factographer of industrial labour in England and the romantic redeemer of vanishing skills of the gypsy and flamenco cultures in Spain, foreground yet another set of urgent contemporary questions: how desirable, even accessible, is the traditional grounding of the contemporary artist in the geo-political formation of the nation state under the impact of an irreversible and continuously accelerating economic globalisation? To what extent is the mythical embeddedness and presumed loyalty to nation state culture, or the acceptance of a deeper determination by its unfathomable definitions of the subject's behavioural and communicative patterns, now merely a hindrance and a handicap to cultural production? Or is it in fact a condition without which communicative cultural practices will wither away and disappear in phantasmic fusions with the apparatuses of the global culture industry (Jeff Koons and Takashi Murakami, as two examples). While they originate in two distinctly different cultural formations, both obey and exacerbate the seemingly inescapable law of a mimetic assimilation to all and every facet of subjective experience to the seemingly glamorous, yet actually violent and rigorous control and octroi of the international fashion and consumption industries and their organised marketing of desire.

It is of course typical that in all the enthusiastic acclaim given to these practices, one question is never even raised, namely: to what extent can the violent internationalism of artistic practices, modelled on the simulacrum of a global idiom, generate its seemingly irresistible power of seduction, only because of its multiple and persistent techniques of obliterating class and effacing the conditions of labour? Not only does it erase the specificities of difference according to gender, ethnicity, race, religion and nation state, but most importantly – and accordingly least addressed – it performs the mythical elimination of class differences under the auspices of a universal egalitarianism of consumption. After all, only when even the faintest trace of a reflection on class can be purged from aesthetic experience, can the simulacrum of a universal egalitarian access to consumption be violently enforced. It seems that this has become in the present one of the central ideological missions of certain highly visible artistic projects.

Lange's tragic artistic and geo-political identity was splintered in at least three ways. Initially there was the New Zealand subject developing a visual archaeology of the rapidly disappearing old industrial foundations of the UK (the coal mining collieries of Nottinghamshire and the steel mills of Bradford among others). Thus in his early work Lange traced the origins and persistence of the industrial culture of the British Commonwealth, the forces that had colonised his own country of origin, yet the coloniser that had also offered him an artistic education at the Royal College of Art in London. Then, in a second major work phase, Lange would devote his time to the exploration of obsolete and historically almost archaic forms of agricultural practices in his beloved geo-political counter space of rural Cantavieja in Spain. [12] And lastly, in regular returns to New Zealand, Lange would develop his investigations of the work forms and labour conditions among the native Māori population, eventually leading to his increasingly politically activist participation in the Māori land reclamation projects.

Thus it is not surprising to find that Lange's work originated at that very moment when the global exportation of labour became one of the essential strategies for rapid profit maximisation in the United States and European economies. At the very moment when an intensifying global campaign on deskilling labour became integral to its perpetual shifting and dislocation, according to rapidly altering markets and distribution systems, Darcy Lange

12 Lange commented on Andalusia as follows: "The remarkable geometric rows and hills, plains and mountain sides of Mediterranean olives stretch out for as far as the eye can see. Perfect parallel rows of trees that curve with the contours of the hills remind one of the intelligent, algebraic thought of Arabia, as well as dealing with the semi-desert of Andalusia. It is tragic that the American advisors and tractors provided to feudal estates have cut the olives, turned Andalusia into a desert, and denied the right to work to thus beautiful Andalusian towns. They did it as if to take the last breath of Andalusian life from the people. These rich landlords buried Andalusia with the death of their hero General Franco. Andalusia, after two thousand years of olives, is nearly a desert now." Lange, op. cit., p. 65.

would construct haunting images of the seemingly primitive activity of a singular Spanish farm worker scything a field.[13] The body in the rhythm of the task-oriented performance, the sure-handedness, the almost balletic elegance of the execution of what would appear to be an excruciatingly exhausting plight, are performed (and recorded by Lange) with an elegance and consonance with the given necessities that give the work both the heroism and the realism of the great exceptional moments when modernism dared to depict labour: ranging from the radical beauty of Gustave Courbet's *Stonebreakers* to Georges Seurat's small, yet monumental sketches of field workers, to Alice Lex Nerlinger's aerial photographs of men fitting a mosaic of stones to build yet another road.

There was ultimately, even if involuntarily, a biographical synthesis of these conflicts in Lange's existence. Just as Marcel Duchamp had declared a manifest dialectical tension by constructing his female alter ego, Rrose Sélavy, to accommodate the irrepressible condition of a subject suspended between the discourses of fashion production and consumption and his 'true' subjectivity of the male artistic producer, so did Lange integrate the conflict between an aesthetic of realist and referential instrumentalisation and an aesthetic of ludic autonomy in the artist's life itself. Following his life-long passion for learning and performing Spanish flamenco music, Lange eventually adopted the name and role of a quite accomplished guitar performer, appearing in concerts as Paco Campana.

In his video recording, *Musicians at Work*, this synthesis is even achieved within the artist's work itself, since Lange appears both as the 'artist' and as the 'worker', i.e. the performing musician within a group of other musicians exercising their artistic and artisan skills. While it might have been more difficult to read and recognise the rhythmic organisation of bodily movement in the farm labourer's activities, working with a primitive scythe in a field, rhythm and repetition as articulations of bodily experience and energetic flows are compelling in the observation of practising musicians. And while it might even have been more unfathomable for most spectators to accept Lange's reflections on the bodily performance of labour as contributions to the ongoing contemplation of what and how sculpture could be productively defined and conceived in the present, Lange's *Musicians at Work* bridges the gap between Bruce Nauman's playing the violin in

13   *Cantavieja, Study of Work in a Spanish Village, Spain,* 1975.

the studio as a radical revision of the sculptural confinement and specific objects, materials and production procedures more compellingly, easing the epistemological transition perhaps even for the most entrenched dogmatics of what sculpture should, can or could not possibly be.

Work Studies, 1973–5

*A Documentation of Calverton and
Pleasley Coalmining Communities,
Nottingham, UK*, 1973

Miners leaving the pit shaft.

A Documentation of Calverton and
Pleasley Coalmining Communities,
Nottingham, UK, 1973

Calverton Colliery.

A Documentation of Calverton and
Pleasley Coalmining Communities,
Nottingham, UK, 1973

Miners coming off shift.

A Documentation of Calverton and
Pleasley Coalmining Communities,
Nottingham, UK, 1973

↑   Miners on break.
→   Playing Cards.
→   Pleasley Colliery Band rehearsal in band
      room, a few yards from the pithead.

A Documentation of Bradford Working Life, UK, 1974

The First Situation: Osborne Steels Ltd.
← 1st Study: 'Rolling Mill'.
← 2nd Study: 'The Grinding'.
← 3rd Study: 'Furnaces'.

The Second Situation: Whiteheads Woollen Mills.
→ 1st Study: 'French Combing'.
→ 2nd Study: 'Traditional Combing'.
→ 4th Study: 'Spinning'.

A Documentation of Bradford Working Life, UK, 1974

The Third Situation: Hepworth and Grandage Ltd.
1st Study: 'The Verson Press'.
2nd Study: 'Piston Inspection'.
3rd Study: 'Dual Lathes'.

A Documentation of Bradford Working
Life, UK, 1974

The Fourth Situation: Grattan Ltd.
← 1st Study: 'Study of a Packer'.
← 2nd Study: 'Study of a Packer'.
← 3rd Study: 'Order Assembly'.
↗ 4th Study: 'Order Assembly'.
↗ 5th Study: 'Punch Card Operator'.

A Documentation of Bradford Working Life, UK, 1974

The Third Situation: Hepworth and Grandage Ltd.
2nd Study: 'Piston Inspection'.

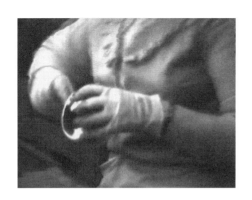

Craigdarrock, Scotland, 1973

Jack Jury, Stockman, Uruti, Taranaki, 1974

*Ruatoria, Study of Sheep Gathering and a
Māori Shearing Gang, East Coast*, 1974

Waitara Freezing Works, Taranaki, 1974

Mutton Chain 1

Beef Conveyor 2

Mutton Chain 3

Stomach Removal

Beef Conveyor 1

Boning Calves

Hewa, Study of a Māori Tree-feller at
Waitaanga, King Country, 1974

Vern Hume, Aerial Top Dressing, Taranaki, 1974

Cantavieja, Study of Work in a Spanish
Village, Spain, 1975

Scything Greens

Wheat Gathering by Mule

Ploughing with Cows

The Village Harvester

Scything Wheat

Preface to the Introduction of the 1977 *Work Studies in Schools* Catalogue[1]

Guy Brett

Since Darcy Lange held his videotape exhibition *Work Studies in Schools* at the Museum of Modern Art in Oxford in 1977, and the essay reprinted here was published in the catalogue, 'screens' have proliferated in our lives to an extraordinary degree. Daily we are exposed to screens on every scale from the mobile phone, through the computer and plasma screen to the huge electronic hoardings of city-centre advertising (just the other day I noticed that the placards which line the escalators in London's Underground have been replaced in some stations by animated LCD screens of exactly the same size and shape, producing – at least until it becomes routine – a potentially maddening derangement of eye and brain). Today, screens, whatever their scale, are junctures of vast and continually growing streams of information coming from all kinds of sources, abutting and overlaying one another, and forcing us to continually shift our attention.

Artists' engagement with new visual technologies has usually been a mixture of excitement and wariness. A fascination with new forms of beauty and the ingenuity of artifice has struggled with a kind of loyalty to 'human value' at its most naked, essential, even archaic. The Quasi-Cinema experiments of the Brazilian artist Hélio Oiticica in the early 1970s were attempts to loosen the hypnotic hold of the projection screen on the spectator. He devised various playful scenarios in which people would lie about in hammocks or on sandy slopes listening to the collage of music and other sounds and watching slide projections which themselves presented the image as a continuous cosmetic 'make-over'. Similarly the American Dan Graham has built transparent and reflective viewing environments that subtly mix individual solitude and social interchange. One could view the whole phenomenon of 'performance' by artists over recent decades as a particular kind of riposte to the omnipresence of recording media. An artist's performance, whether it was electronically recorded or

1   Published by the Museum of Modern Art in Oxford in 1977, to accompany Lange's exhibition there.

not, was a unique event in time and space, was un-recordable, and its future willingly submitted to the vagaries of human memory (including the artist's!).

Viewing today some of the videotapes Darcy Lange made in the UK in the 1970s inevitably makes one reflect on the effects of the passage of time. In a sense the work processes he filmed, in all their material specificity (matter, sound, space, movement – impressed on us so intensely by Lange's artistic method) and the technical means of recording them, the cumbersome early video equipment, have aged together. This involves the surface, the fairly obvious ways in which what was once 'present' has become 'past', which could well, as time continues to pass, become a valuable record for historians and sociologists. But what has not faded in this sense is the point at which Lange's excitement with the possibilities of the new medium meets and merges with his desire to get closer through his art to life and to people.

The possibilities that excited me too – the long unedited take, the fixed viewpoint, instant playback and its effects on those filmed, multiple screen installations, a new experience of watching – have retained their potency and critical edge through the 30 intervening years of media development. And, perhaps, by viewing today Lange's individual manner of using them has become clearer too. There was a lot more to it than simply switching on the camera and letting it run (though this basic gesture still applies).

At the beginning of one of the tapes made inside Bradford factories in the mid-1970s, industrial noise floods in as the questing eye roams over the messy fabric of the workshop in close-up detail – wood, steel, brick – and then after a time, just in the course of things without fanfare, comes upon a man's working back. In his studies of people at work Lange never separates one person out as a hero or emblem of Labour, not does he look for 'personality'. The essential relationship is between people and their environment, which may be seen in close-up or far distant. In one of the tapes made around the village of Cantavieja in Spain in 1975, the shepherdess is not seen in any detail until right near the end of the filming. Before then she has been a tiny figure in the distance marshalling a flock of sheep and goats and shepherding them through the immense landscape. In Lange's tapes people have time. They pass in and out of the frame, they move about in the space they occupy rather than in an author's space of a narrative, symbolic or interrogatory kind.

Preface to the Introduction of the 1977 *Work Studies in Schools* Catalogue

Though Darcy Lange was not given to theoretical argument, 'realism' was clearly a major question for him. On the one hand he espoused a notion of realism as "unselfish and unromantic observation of people and their hard but tranquil and troubled existence". At the same time realism could be an adjunct of power over people, and he identified this in what he called "Roman realism" (perhaps having in mind the portrait busts of Roman senators and generals with their aura of worldly ambition, of governing and calculating, which we seem to read in the lines of their faces). By contrast Lange was drawn to "other cultures" and their opposition to "perfect imitation": cultures that developed symbolism, and even the abstraction of textile forms, where "the artist's imagination made a larger contribution". He looked critically at his own instrument – the camera which, he speculated, may "strip the people of their spiritual prestige". "Are we meant to reproduce exactly? Are we meant to destroy the poetic approximations which existed before the realities of science?" [2] These last two questions become poignant and revealing of Lange's attitude given his adherence to a scrupulous observation.

The work Lange did in the UK came during a decade of intense politicisation among artists. It was an 'activist' moment, which saw the formation of many groups and artistic practices dedicated to new forms of social intervention. Groups like APG (Artists Placement Group, started by John Latham and Barbara Steveni, to place artists as 'incidental persons' in factories, hospitals and bureaucratic departments), Artists for Democracy (a broad front cultural centre started by David Medalla), The Women's Art Alliance and others, and individual bodies of work like Peter Kennard's anti-nuclear photomontages, Jo Spence's feminist performance photography, John Dugger's banners, Derek Boshier's graphic work (and the exhibition, *Lives*, he organised at the Hayward Gallery in London which included a 50 minute Darcy Lange video) are some pointers to a period of extra-institutional activity and audacity.

Darcy Lange's *Work Studies* were produced in this context but were fired, or inflected, by his individual history. Having grown up on a farm in New Zealand, a country with relative social equality, he was astonished by the "incredible class system which still prevails in England". [3] This probably drove him to leave London and make his tapes of farmers, miners, factory workers and teachers (the Oxford tapes are shot through with subtle evidence of class

2   Darcy Lange, *Video Art*, The Department of Film, Television and Media Studies, University of Auckland, Auckland, 2001, p. 16.

3   Darcy Lange in an interview with Willoughby Sharp, *Avalanche*, Summer 1975, p. 12.

distinctions). But perhaps, for Lange personally, the great divide of loyalties in his own life was between his video camera and his guitar, between his intense scrutiny of the visible world and losing himself in the timeless flamenco.

Reminiscing recently, David Elliott, who was director of the Museum of Modern Art in Oxford in 1977 and commissioned the *Work Studies in Schools*, gave a moving account of how the exhibition came to be made and his own assessment of its significance. By way of introduction to the reprinted text I would like to quote him in some detail:

> Darcy Lange's *Work Studies in Schools* was one of the first shows I programmed as Director of the Museum of Modern Art Oxford and it was designed to kill three birds with one stone: the first was to commission an important piece using the still relatively new medium of video by one of the leading artists working in that field in the UK; the second was to build up links with the community around Oxford – not one renowned for its love of or interest in contemporary art; the third was to provide a reflection, and through this a critique, of divergent attitudes in both art education and society in the public and private sectors. Made during the twilight years of the previous Labour Government, this latter aspect of the work has since acquired a poignancy that we could have hardly anticipated at the time – our notions of what constitutes 'public' and 'private' have now been completely turned on their heads. Who better to create such a materially modest, yet spiritually ambitious work as this than Darcy Lange. His energy, openness and ability to communicate gave this work its unique attraction. This was 'real life' – cinema verité if you like – but through a prism of innocent enthusiasm that completely negated the reflexive post-structuralist approach of so many video artists of the time, as well as the potential boredom of its grisaille medium. Darcy's work transcended the specificity of each school to give a portrait of adolescence and control to which we could all relate. [4]

4   David Elliott, email to the author,
     1 April 2007. Quoted with the writer's
     kind permission.

Study of Three Birmingham Schools, UK, 1976

Ladywood Comprehensive School.

DARCY LANGE
WORK STUDIES IN SCHOOLS

22 MARCH — 9 APRIL
TUESDAY - SATURDAY 10 - 5, SUNDAY 2 - 5, MONDAY CLOSED

Museum of Modern Art Oxford

30 Pembroke Street Oxford OX1 1BP 0865 722733

Exhibition poster for *Work Studies in Schools* at the Museum of Modern Art Oxford, 1977.

Reprint of the Introduction to the 1977 *Work Studies in Schools* Catalogue

Guy Brett

These videotapes should not be seen as a finished and completed work. Darcy Lange describes them as 'researches'. The ones in this exhibition, which are studies of teaching of different subjects in comprehensive and public schools, are only the latest he has made on the general theme of studies of people at work. In the last few years he has made videotapes in a Nottinghamshire mining village, in Bradford, in Spain, and in his own country New Zealand (a full list is printed on page 6). It is hard to say what final form this accumulation of material could take.

Darcy Lange is searching for ways to make the best possible use of his tapes even while continuing to make them. A set-up like this in a gallery, with a number of separate viewing rooms and chairs, is only provisional, for nobody knows quite how to categorise this kind of work. Particularly important for the artist in knowing how to develop this work further are the reactions of audiences; both the people participating in the tapes when they see them played back afterwards, and different individuals and groups among the public. An exhibition in an art gallery naturally puts the emphasis on the artist, the author. But in this case the emphasis should fall on the project, and what is revealed by it.

'People at work' has often been a theme treated by documentary photographers and film-makers. Lange acknowledges his links with them and also uses still photography and film. But something quite new is brought to the subject by the use of videotape. Video in the way Lange has used it has been able to reveal new aspects of the relation of people to their work, and to stimulate new feelings and questions in the audience. This is tied up with its peculiar possibilities and limitation as a medium.

For instance, videotape is not easy to cut and to edit; and therefore many properties we are used to in films are missing in these tapes. There is no montage, no building up of sequences. There is no easy way of shooting different things going on simultaneously, or the same thing from different angles, and adding them together to form a whole afterwards. But what's missing in drama and orchestration is repaid with a kind of steady observation. The behaviour and movement of people and things really impresses itself on us because time passes at the same speed on the screen as it does for us, watching.

In some ways Lange has returned to a more primitive and static use of the camera. When a tape starts we find ourselves all at once in a particular place, with particular people, a particular camera position. All the background noise floods in. Work is in progress. The camera may not move for a long time, or if it does, it moves very slowly sideways or with a gradual use of the zoom. In the study of *Spinning* made at Whiteheads Woollen Mill, Bradford, there is time for the complexity and power of the machine to make a strong impression, and the relationship of Mrs. Alice Jennings to it as she walks backwards and forwards endlessly adjusting the threads, to become very clear.

By sacrificing the power to synthesise, to bring in outside elements, to construct his film after the event, Lange puts his camera more in the position of a person watching. He has no special vantage-point. In the classroom tapes, the camera doesn't dart restlessly here and there trying to pick up every incident, but tends to move slowly, almost ruminatively, about the room, relying on the voices on the sound-track to give continuity.

Another peculiarity of video is that it can be played back instantly, if necessary in the same place with the same equipment. Many practical possibilities flowing from this have been seized on. The simple distancing of a person from himself or herself can have a profound therapeutic effect. People who have injured themselves for example make quicker recoveries when they can see tapes of how they were a few days before.

This quality of video can change the activity of documentary-making and draw its boundaries in a new way. The people originally filmed can comment on the tape, give their reflections and criticisms and this becomes incorporated into the work itself. Thus its relationship to reality can become more active and also in a way more humorous. A criticism of the means of representation is included too. The form of Lange's documentary is suggested by this technical fact of video. The studies of teaching all follow the same schema: a tape of teaching in the classroom, a tape of the teacher at home, discussions with the students and teachers after the first tapes have been made, and also interviews with outsiders who have a special interest. There's no reason it couldn't be extended further.

This emphasis on some of the technical aspects of video is not to suggest that the artist is interested in them for their own sake or merely wants to exploit them for new effects, but in order to see what attitude to life they enable him to express.

Earlier, Lange worked as a sculptor. But he abandoned this field because he felt the very activity isolated him. He couldn't see a real use in it. In an essay at the time he wrote: "Unfortunately my artistic life has been mostly spent in an institution (art school). I feel it is immensely important to spend much time involving myself with real people and real problems of life." He adopted film and video as a means of getting closer to 'real people'. But not merely as subject-matter. To try to end his isolation the artist searches also for his audience, he tries to redefine his activity in relation to the public in a new way to bring himself closer to the people. This is a very difficult problem.

Darcy Lange aimed to extend the quality he admired in the earlier documentary photographers such as Lewis Hine or Dorothea Lange of "unselfish and unromantic observation of people and their hard but tranquil and troubled existence". He felt they had an attitude of integrity and considerateness towards those they photographed. In his tapes Lange has neither filmed people secretly without their knowledge, nor manipulated them for the sake of drama or composition. At the same time he hasn't used reality gratuitously for the sake of some abstract 'structural' project. He would like to put into filming the same time, observation and love for the person as Van Gogh put into one of his drawings of a textile worker or an old man. The meaning of this effort by an artist to overcome alienation can be felt by comparing Lange's tapes with the way the same subject is treated by the mass media, especially by television – the identical medium. Despite their apparent casualness, his long takes of people working are a passionate criticism of television. They show, by contrast, how television never gives us time to observe things properly, to reflect and think, to meet on equal terms with the persons or situation represented so that we might relate them to our own lives. They show the frenzied way reality is chopped up and packaged by TV for our passive consumption.

Lange himself says that he is trying to observe the environment without manipulating it, to present it directly to the audience. He counters the highly sophisticated manipulative techniques of the mass media with a kind of primitivism. His tapes give you the feeling of 'being there' in a kind of elementary, naïve fashion. Because the tapes are not cut, not edited to follow an argument or produce an entertainment, you are both brought very close to the subject and also paradoxically distanced from it. For me these videotapes brought home what it's like to work in a factory, made me think about the process of 'education' – better than many documentaries where the arguments are set out and systematised. This modest procedure of observing and 'distancing' from everyday life can carry with it a surprising force, because it can lead to the making of comparisons.

At the same time the idea of 'non-manipulation', if it is taken too far, can become the opposite. It can turn into an attitude of neutrality and indifference, a sort of aesthetic phantom, because there is no such pure state of non-manipulation. The artist is always forced to make choices. And whatever he or she produces is going to be seen differently by different individuals and groups within the audience. The tape of a worker operating a steel press is going to be seen differently by workers in the factory, than by someone who has never been inside a factory. Teachers will see the classroom tapes in a different way from the students. For some people, even the unpretentious style of filming will seem like just the opposite and will be difficult to pay attention to, in the same way that for some, to be photographed 'informally' without being prepared and properly arranged before the camera, means a loss of human dignity. All this bears on the relation between the artist's point of view, the point of view of the subject, and of the audience. All these influence each other, 'manipulate' each other.

In his book *The Camera and I* the great documentary film-maker Joris Ivens described the transformation brought about in this work by the experience of showing his films to audiences in the revolutionary atmosphere of the early years of the Soviet Union. Up till then he had been mainly concerned with the aesthetic problems and possibilities of film.

> The Soviet audiences I talked to were made up of film workers, scientists, factory workers, aviation officers and many other groups ... After the films would come the most surprising questions and criticism. There are audiences who

Reprint of the Introduction to the 1977 *Work Studies in Schools* Catalogue look at your work on the screen and listen to what you have to say and then leave. Not so the Soviet audiences – they always want to know more.

"They always want to know more" – this is a challenge for the artist to overcome his preciousness and work more truly.

Study of Three Birmingham Schools, UK, 1976

Study of Three Birmingham Schools, UK, 1976

Mrs. Hunter, 'Teaching the Infants',
Leabank Junior School.

Study of Three Birmingham Schools, UK, 1976

Mr. Perks, 'Animal Farm', English Class,
Ladywood Comprehensive School.

Study of Three Birmingham Schools, UK, 1976

Mr. Rigby, Biology Class, King Edward's School.

Study of Three Birmingham Schools, UK, 1976

Mr. Perks, Mr. Brendon and students
discussing the recording,
Ladywood Comprehensive School.

Mr. Brendon, 'Teacher Response',
Ladywood Comprehensive School.

Study of Three Birmingham Schools, UK, 1976

'The Theatre Group', King Edward's School.

Study of Three Birmingham Schools, UK, 1976

Mr. Hughes, 'The Wheel', Leabank
Junior School.

Study of Three Birmingham Schools, UK, 1976

Mr. Trott, English Literature and Language
class, Webster, King Edward's School.

Study of Three Birmingham Schools, UK, 1976

Mr. Hughes interview, Leabank
Junior School.

Exacting Reproduction: Darcy Lange's *Work Studies in Schools*

Lawrence McDonald

Darcy Lange was trained as a fine artist, not as a camera artist (film, video and photography): nor was he trained as a social scientist. Yet by using his camera(s) to observe and investigate many of the classic topics of social enquiry, he made the work upon which his reputation as an artist rests. The purpose of this essay is to discuss how a major part of this work, specifically the studies made in various English schools during 1976–7, connects with contemporaneous and subsequent developments in cultural studies and the ethnography of the classroom.

Darcy Lange's turn from the formalist concerns of late modernist, geometric hard-edged sculpture and, following that, multi-media sculptural installations, to film, photography and, above all, video studies of the social world parallels that of a number of other artists at work in the late 1960s and early 1970s. For instance, Conrad Atkinson, who in the early/middle 1960s "... was trained at the Royal Academy under a very traditional fine arts curriculum",[1] but abandoned formalist painting for politically conscious art. In 1972, London's ICA (Institute of Contemporary Arts) hosted Atkinson's exhibition *Strike*, "... which brought me out of this studio-art-school-gallery cocoon into realism",[2] and it also showed his 1974 exhibition *Work, Wages and Prices*. It is important to note that the period in which this work was made – and also Lange's *A Documentation of Calverton and Pleasley Coalmining Communities, Nottingham, UK* (1973) and his *A Documentation of Bradford Working Life, UK* (1974) – gave rise to waves of working class militancy directed against the Conservative Government of Edward Heath. In his diagnosis of the political implications of Heath's policies, Robin Blackburn asserted: "... Heath is preparing the ground for the birth, or re-birth, of revolutionary politics within the working class. In terms of the British class struggle this would represent perhaps as significant an advance for British workers as the possibilities of May 1968 represented in terms of the French class struggle for French workers."[3]

1 Timothy Rollins, 'Art as Social Action: an Interview with Conrad Atkinson', in *Art in America*, vol. 68, no. 2, February 1980, p. 121.

2 Richard Cork, 'Conrad Atkinson: Interview', in *Studio International*, vol. 191, no. 980, March/April 1976, p. 179. The exhibition *A Century of Artists' Films in Britain* (Tate Gallery, 19 May to 10 August 2003) showed a 10 minute section of Lange's film *Osborn Steels Ltd Bradford* (1974) in the 'Work' programme, alongside Conrad Atkinson's *Industrial Relations Bill* (1971), 3mins. A programme note stated: "Industrial strife and the political changes in Britain in the early 1970s are reflected in the work of several artists, who used film to explore individual rights and contemporary working conditions".

3 Robin Blackburn, 'The Heath Government: A New Course for British Capitalism' in *New Left Review*, no. 70, November to December 1971, p. 26. Heath's Conservative Government was elected in 1970 with Margaret Thatcher as Secretary of State for Education. Lange's *Work Studies in Schools* were made and first exhibited under a Labour Government. The Conservatives returned to power under Margaret Thatcher in 1979.

But Atkinson's overtly political work was not the only model of an art that attempted to engage with the social world in the early 1970s. Stephen Willats, another English artist, also strived to reach a wider (non-art) audience with works that drew upon studies in social psychology and the sociology of groups. Willats confronted the problem of art's separation from society by addressing broader issues of "social coding structures" beyond what he termed "art's social environment" (i.e. a self-enclosed art world); [4] and to do so he turned to theoretical schemas of cognition and perception within technologically-based, interactive installations such as *Meta Filter* (1975). By contrast, the American-based German artist Hans Haacke's 1970s studies of the machinations of networks of power relationships were focused directly on the art world itself as the most effective site for political intervention. Becker and Walton summarise his work of this period as "... a contribution to social science method by adapting the art historical technique of the provenance to the study of power". [5]

The social science orientation of Darcy Lange's 1970s video studies is more implicit than that of the artists named above but it is manifested in a number of linked ways. The first thing to note is that the overriding preoccupation of these studies is the classic sociological one of work in both urban and rural settings. The former includes the wage labour of factory and colliery work as well as the unpaid recreational work of tending allotment gardens. The latter takes in, amongst other things, the following: the horticultural and pastoral work of a rural peasantry in Cantavieja, Spain; the forestry, shearing, and mustering of a rural proletariat in New Zealand; and the recreational activity of competition axemen in Taranaki, New Zealand. All of these studies are focused on cycles of production, whereas Lange's other major 1970s series, the *Work Studies in Schools* (1976–7), is fundamentally concerned with patterns of reproduction, the manner in which society maintains and renews itself inter-generationally, focusing on the education system as a site where class differences are reinforced or contested. And given that one of the major outcomes of societal reproduction is the maintenance of socio-economic inequality, it isn't surprising that Lange's exclusive concentration on working class and peasant labour in the *Work Studies* expands to include middle class subjects in the school studies. This is not the only difference between these two broad bodies of work. The studies of work tend to restrict themselves to purely observational records of the work process

4   Stephen Willats, 'Art Work as Social Model' in *Studio International*, op.cit., pp. 100–105.

5   Howard S. Becker and John Walton, 'Social Science and the Work of Hans Haacke', in *Hans Haacke, Framing and Being Framed: 7 Works 1970–75*, Halifax: The Press of the Nova Scotia College of Art and Design, 1975, p. 148.

Exacting Reproduction: Darcy Lange's *Work Studies in Schools*

itself. The school studies retain this mode for the documentation of the classroom lesson, but introduce an informal, conversational interview with the teacher concerned (after viewing the classroom tape) and a discussion with a selection of students from the class. These interviews and discussions require Lange's participation as both on- and off-screen presence in a way not seen in the previous *Work Studies*, even though he had contemplated doing something similar in them. Therefore the school studies possess both self-reflexive and interactive dimensions that move them beyond the purely observational mode of the earlier *Work Studies*.

Robert Flaherty's evening screenings of work-in-progress to the subjects of his film *Moana: A Romance of the Golden Age* (1926) is a documentary precedent for this,[6] but no direct trace of the practice was incorporated into the finished film. More directly comparable is Jean Rouch and Edgar Morin's "exercise in cinema-verite", *Chronique d'Été* (*Chronicle of a Summer*, 1960), which begins with a discussion between the film-makers and one of their subjects and moves towards a conclusion with a penultimate scene in which the directors and all the participants in their film discuss the material shot and its implications, after a screening inside a theatre. *Chronicle of a Summer* marked something of a departure from Rouch's earlier African-based films of the 1950s in terms of its setting (the urban society of contemporary Paris) and its use of lightweight, portable 16mm film equipment (Rouch drew upon the expertise of cameraman Michel Brault of the National Film Board of Canada, a pioneer in the use of this equipment). Just over a decade later, Lange was able to benefit from yet another technological breakthrough – the advent of portable, lightweight video equipment, which not only allowed a single operator to handle both picture and sound but also had the added advantage of enabling that operator to provide on-the-spot playback for his subjects. Thus, a one-man 'crew' and the absence of bulky equipment, combined with portability and facility of playback, made it possible for Lange to both work unobtrusively in the classroom and establish a close relationship with his subjects.

Lange conducted his *Work Studies in Schools* in two UK locations, Birmingham (1976) and Oxfordshire (1977), and at several schools within these areas. The three Birmingham schools studied were: Leabank Junior School (i.e. a primary school); Ladywood Comprehensive School; and King Edward's School.[7] The four Oxfordshire schools studied were: Cheney

6   David MacDougall, 'Beyond Observational Cinema' in Paul Hockings (ed.), *Principles of Visual Anthropology*, The Hague/Paris: Mouton Publishers, 1975, pp. 119–20.

7   *Study of Three Birmingham Schools, UK*, 1976.

8   *Studies of Teaching in Four Oxfordshire Schools, UK*, 1977.

9   "In 1969 26.2% of all state secondary pupils were in comprehensive schools. In 1974 this had risen to 62%, and in 1978 the figure was 83%." Stephen Ball, *Education*, London & New York: Longman, 1986, p. 21. Comprehensive schools were founded on what Ball refers to as "the integrative view", which assumes that "… by providing one school for all, with social classes mixed together, greater tolerance and social harmony will result and class tensions will abate". (p. 24).

10   Darcy Lange, 'To Effect a Truthful Study of Work in Schools', in *Work Studies in Schools*, Museum of Modern Art Oxford, 1977, p. 18.

Upper School (comprehensive); St Mary's School (public school, i.e. private); Banbury School (comprehensive); and Radley College (public school, i.e. private). [8] The lessons videotaped in the three Birmingham schools varied from school to school: they were devoted to social studies and music (Leabank), English literature, biology, geology and physics (King Edward's) and geometry, history, physics and shorthand (Ladywood). However, in the Oxfordshire project, Lange settled on recording lessons in art, history, and science (chemistry or biology) across all the schools, with classes ranging from forms three to seven. The mix of public (i.e. private) and state schools (grammar, comprehensive, and primary) that make up Lange's 'sample' of the English education system demonstrates his interest in mapping and correlating class-based differences in educational provision in the 1970s. [9]

A fundamental question to ask of Lange's *Work Studies in Schools* is: what is the purpose behind them? In order to answer this question, we will largely have to make inferences from the tapes themselves because there is very little in the way of extra-artistic statements from Lange to draw upon. However, in an artist's statement, in the catalogue for the first exhibition of the school studies at the Museum of Modern Art Oxford, Lange listed his guidelines for making them as follows:

1. To investigate teaching as work.
2. To illustrate the skills of the teacher through vocal and gestural communication with the class and also the class's response to this.
3. To illustrate the process of teaching and learning in the classroom.
4. To illustrate the social breakdown within each class.
5. I am particularly concerned to prevent what I make, whether it be photograph or video from becoming an end in itself – not dissimilar to the loved art object. [10]

All of these guidelines are clear, with the exception of number four, which is ambiguous. Does it refer to the anatomisation of social differences between pupils in the classes studied or, in a quite different sense of the word 'breakdown', to failures within the process of educational transmission? The first two guidelines focus on the teacher as worker and the relative degree of skill he or she possesses as a communicator. Number five focuses on Lange himself as an artist who wishes to disavow the orthodox role of maker of a self-enclosed object for purely aesthetic contemplation. This leaves guideline number three as the key descriptor of the project's principal aim and the one that aligns it most directly with other, non-visually orientated classroom studies of the period.

In an essay published in 1971, in an influential collection of educational papers, Basil Bernstein isolated three crucial dimensions underpinning educational knowledge: curriculum; pedagogy; and evaluation. The first "defines what is valid knowledge", the second "what counts as a valid transmission of knowledge", and the third "what counts as a valid realisation of this knowledge on the part of the taught". [11] Which of these dimensions does Lange's work address? It is evident that pedagogy is not only the main focus of the classroom recordings themselves but that discussion of it also dominates the subsequent interviews with the teachers. Lange does occasionally pose questions of curriculum and evaluation during the teacher interviews but they receive far less attention than pedagogy, which is reflected upon intensively. To a large degree, curriculum and evaluation remain 'hidden' within the tapes and it becomes the task of the viewer to excavate them or infer them by reading between the lines.

In the UK throughout the 1970s, there was a concerted shift on the part of some educational researchers towards direct observation of classroom practices. To varying degrees, these researchers turned towards the anthropological methodology of ethnography in order to gain inside knowledge of teacher-student dynamics. They elected to become participant-observers by taking up residence in classrooms for long periods of time. In this section of the essay, I want to look at a number of studies made at a similar time and place to Lange's in order to contextualise and throw light on his practice. [12]

The first study I want to consider is also the one closest to Lange's in its classroom focus on the relationship between teacher expectation and pupil attainment in various UK primary schools and the secondary school that subsequently takes many of the pupils involved. The theoretical orientation behind Roy Nash's *Classrooms Observed* (1973) is derived from social psychology but its methodology is unusual for this orientation in being based on participant-observation. Nash stresses the need for this kind of research to clearly identify the object of the study, be properly analytic in procedure and be systematic in the compiling of notes

11   Basil Bernstein, 'On the Classification and Framing of Educational Knowledge' in M. F. D. Young (ed.), *Knowledge and Control: New Directions for the Sociology of Education*, London: Routledge and Kegan Paul, 1971, p. 47.

12   Lange's library contained a number of books on educational topics: James D. Koerner, *The Miseducation of American Teachers,* Baltimore: Penguin Books, 1963, bought in a bookstore in Harlem, NYC; Neil Postman and Charles Weingartner, *Teaching as a Subversive Activity*, Penguin Books, 1972; and Charles Silberman, *Crisis in the Classroom, the Making of American Education*, New York: Vintage Books, 1970. But amongst these, the book most directly related to the concerns of his own practice is Rob Walker and Clem Adelman's *A Guide to Classroom Observation*, London: Methuen and Co Ltd., 1975, a guide and resource book designed for prospective teachers undertaking the "transitional role" of observer in the classrooms of experienced teachers. It addresses general issues of observational practice such as: how to react to a class; where to sit; degree of participation in the class; analysis of the teacher's gesture, voice and movement; analysis of the pupils' reactions; and how teachers' observations can serve to modify their own teaching strategies. It also discusses various "aids to observation", including different methods of recording such as audiotape, videotape, and slides. The authors emphasise that "the essence of observation is the creation of insight out of what might seem initially to be routine and commonplace" (p. 18).

and indexes. "The problem of structuring field notes", he writes, "is one of the principal problems of participant observation. The temptation for the inexperienced worker is to try to note everything." [13] Yet no matter how comprehensive an observer's field notes might strive to be, I would emphasise that they will always be a selective rendering of a particular observer's experience of the classroom by means of the conventions of social science reporting. However, when the participant-observer takes a video camera into the field, the question of the relationship between 'field notes' and analysis becomes considerably more complicated. I will return to this matter later in the essay, after examining another contribution to the ethnography of the classroom.

Perhaps the most important and influential of the 1970s UK-based studies that employed ethnography as its principal methodology is Paul Willis's *Learning to Labour: How Working Class Kids Get Working Class Jobs* (1977). [14] When he carried out the research and wrote up the results for this study, Willis was a member of the Centre for Contemporary Cultural Studies at the University of Birmingham. However, even though theories of ethnography were an important component of the Centre's general intellectual orientation, particularly in relation to the study of sub-cultural identities and resistance, *Learning to Labour* is the only large-scale and sustained use of ethnography in the Centre's canon. Furthermore, Willis's work stands somewhat apart from the more abstracted neo-Gramscian approach of the Centre in its emphasis on sensuous, lived relations embodied in socio-symbolic practices. [15]

Learning to Labour provides an in-depth case study of Hammertown Boys, a fictional name for a (then) boys-only secondary modern school in the Midlands. Willis focuses on a core group of 12 non-academic students at a school whose entire intake was working class. These 12 boys form a group of "lads", which constitutes itself as a "counter-school culture" in opposition to the conformist "ear 'oles" who please teachers by striving for academic success. Willis's research explores the lads' attitudes, responses and resistance towards schooling and how their "counter-school culture" steers them directly to their preferred post-school destination of "shop floor culture". [16] Thus, he demonstrates how their rituals simultaneously resist the educational priorities of the school and serve to secure their (self) reproduction as another generation of working class labourers. [17]

13 Roy Nash, *Classrooms Observed: The Teacher's Perception and the Pupil's Performance*, London and Boston: Routledge & Kegan Paul, 1973, p. 45. About five years after completing this study, Nash took up a lecturership in the Education Department of Massey University in Palmerston North, New Zealand. Between taking up that position and his death in 2006, Professor Nash established himself as a leading sociologist of education.

14 Paul Willis, *Learning to Labour: How Working Class Kids Get Working Class Jobs*, Aldershot, Hampshire: Gower, 1980, 81, 83 (reprinted). First published by Saxon House, 1977.

15 The Centre for Contemporary Cultural Studies' major publication on education is the Education Group's multi-authored historical and theoretical study *Unpopular Education: Schooling and Social Democracy in England Since 1944*, London: Hutchinson, 1981.

16 Willis discusses "shop floor culture" in 'Human Experience and Material Production: the Culture of the Shop Floor' in *Working Papers in Cultural Studies 9*, Spring 1976, pp. 154–161. This article is an extract from a lecture related to work completed for a project with the title 'The Transition from School to Work'.

17 Here I'm playing on the title of a major Birmingham Centre collection of writing on sub-cultural resistance – *Resistance through Rituals*, edited by Stuart Hall and Tony Jefferson, London: Hutchinson, 1976.

As mentioned already, Willis's principal methodology in his classroom studies was participant-observation ethnography. Within this particular orientation, the technological device used by Willis for the recording of encounters with his subjects was the audiotape recorder. The only visual aspect of his study is the cover of the published book. I'm familiar with two different editions. The first, an American edition, published by Columbia University Press Morningside in 1981, carries a single photograph by Stuart Haden of the exterior of a furniture factory. This stark image of an aged brick building signals immediately Willis's emphasis on the direct link between work and school, an emphasis shared by Lange, who not only moved between work and school studies but also chose to emphasise the link by calling the latter *Work Studies in Schools*. And, whether intended or not, this cover image also brings to mind Bertolt Brecht's well known statement about photography, quoted by Walter Benjamin as follows:

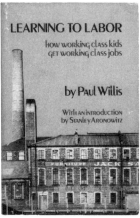

> The situation is complicated by the fact that less than ever does the mere reflection of reality reveals anything about reality. A photograph of the Krupp works or the AEG tells us next to nothing about these institutions. Actual reality has slipped into the functional. The reification of human relations – the factory, say – means that they are no longer explicit. So something must in fact be built up, something artificial, posed.[18]

It is the task of Willis's book to show how social relations developed inside the school play a determining role in the reproduction of social relations behind the factory facade represented in the cover photograph. He does this in large part by means of the analysis of transcripts of his conversations with the lads.

    The other edition of *Learning to Labour*, published by Gower (1980, reprinted 1981, 1983), has a quite different cover. It contains a set of photographs, by Roy Peters and Willis himself, most of which, presumably, were taken during the period of his research. The cover is bisected by a red horizontal band in the form of a filmstrip or a series of juxtaposed television screens. Above the band, occupying the top-third of the cover is a black and white photograph of a sprawling factory complex towering over a rank of terrace houses. The book's subtitle is superimposed in red over this photograph in the top left-hand corner, and diagonal to this

18 Walter Benjamin, 'Little History of Photography' in *Selected Writings Volume Two, Part Two 1931–1934*, translated by Rodney Livingstone et al. & edited by Michael W. Jennings et al., Cambridge, MA & London: Harvard University Press, 1999, p. 526.

is Willis's name. Below the band is a somewhat larger photograph of two children, shot from behind, walking across (industrial?) wasteland, presumably on their way to school? Superimposed on this image, in very large red type, is the book's main title. Inside the central band's frames or screens are school photographs: two of them taken inside classrooms, the other two, one of which is cut off by the cover's edge, in the school playground. Unlike the abstracted and stylised photograph of the factory on the cover of the Columbia University Press edition (the cover design adds a magenta tint to the photograph), all these photographs are very much in the vein of social documentary images: stark, unadorned and captured 'on the fly'. The school pictures could be frame grabs from any number of Lange's *Work Studies in Schools*.

Like Willis, Lange strived to integrate himself unobtrusively into the classrooms he studied, even though his video equipment prevented him from blending seamlessly into the rows of students' desks. With the exception of the earlier Birmingham studies (e.g. Mr. Hughes in Leabank and Mr. Trott in King Edward's) where he placed himself at the front of the class, the viewpoint of his camera is usually from the back and side of the classroom. [19] However, regardless of where he is situated, it is clear that his video camera and ongoing videographic activity gave Lange a clearly defined role in the classroom that helped to contribute to the acceptance of his presence by both teachers and pupils. [20] The first phase of Lange's studies, the recording of classroom lessons, conforms closely to the dictates of observational ethnographic documentary. The second phase, incorporating both individual teacher interviews and discussions with selected pupils, is comparable to Willis's informal interviews and is dialogical in nature. As previously stated, it is this second phase that distinguishes *Work Studies in Schools* from Lange's purely observational studies of work processes in factories. It enables teachers and, to a lesser degree, students to reflect upon their lessons and allows Lange to ask questions and make comments of his own. But does it contain the kind of higher order analysis and synthesis achieved by Willis in his written ethnography? This is a fundamental question facing any ethnographic documentary, but particularly those that work predominantly within the observational mode. Willis's field notes and his raw and transcribed audiotapes constitute the data he took from the field. The only direct traces of this data within the published book are quoted extracts from his interview transcripts.

19 This is in line with Walker and Adelman's recommendation that "generally you want to be in a position where you can observe but intrude least in the activities of the class". This avoids the problem of "distracting the pupils" but "also means you cannot see their faces". To alleviate this they suggest sitting "... to one side so that you can at least see something of the children's faces". *A Guide to Classroom Observation*, London: Methuen and Co. Ltd., 1975, p. 18.

20 Frequently in his follow-up interview sessions with teachers and pupils, Lange poses questions on the extent to which his videotaping interferes with the authenticity or honesty of the teachers' and pupils' performances and their level of awareness of his presence. It is clear that he wished to minimise these effects and adhere strictly to the objective nature of the observational mode.

Exacting Reproduction: Darcy Lange's *Work Studies in Schools*

By contrast, Lange's videotapes are both research data (document) and finished study (documentary) at once. There is no moment of separation between data collection and interpretative processing, as there is in Willis's shaping of his field materials for educational and cultural studies readerships. And given the sheer scale of Lange's project, the only means of delivery to a non-specialist audience is via curatorial intervention in the form of rigorous selection and editing. What would serve to distinguish the moment of research in the field from the moment of a self-evidently crafted and finished study is, in the first instance, the practice of editing and, secondly, recourse to the incorporation of such second-order processing devices as voice-over commentary, titling or more extensive written text, and sound design. None of the features listed second is present in any of Lange's tapes; and editing is, at most, minimal if not entirely absent. One reason for this is the difficulty of and limited capacity for editing videotape in the 1970s. However, the main reason is Lange's long take, observational aesthetic, which traces the unfolding of social processes in real time without interruption.

Thus, measured against an ideal set of criteria for the making of ethnographic documentary – for instance those adumbrated by Karl Heider – Lange's videos score highly in some areas and not so well in others. [21] On the one hand, he demonstrates: "basic technical competence"; "minimal inadvertent or intentional distortion of behaviour"; "ethnographic presence" (he is "shown interacting and gathering data"); little or no "distortion in the film-making process" by preserving actual sequences in real time; 'appropriateness of sound' through the use of "natural synchronous sound"; contextualisation; the framing of whole bodies ("maximally necessary whole bodies"); the recording of "whole acts" ("beginnings, peaks and ends"); the delivery of "whole people" ("develops feeling for an individual"). On the other hand, there is: no "explanation of the various distortions", if any, in the videotapes; no "narration fit", simply because there is no narration in any of the tapes; no "relation to printed materials" because none exists in relation to these purely audio-visual studies; and, finally, it has to be admitted that in the strict anthropological sense these tapes are "uninformed by ethnographic understanding". Furthermore, after glossing his set of attributes of ethnographic film, Heider then ranks them in order of importance within an "attribute dimension grid". Placed at the top are: "ethnographic

21 Karl Heider, *Ethnographic Film*, Austin & London: University of Texas Press, 1976, pp. 98–111.

basis" ("uninformed by ethnography" or "deeply shaped by ethnographic understanding"?), and "relation to printed materials" (moving by degrees from "no printed materials" to "fully integrated with printed materials"). It is precisely these two top ranked attributes against which Lange's tapes score least well. However, as stated at the beginning of this essay, all Lange's *Work Studies* emerged from his trajectory as an artist shifting from formal concerns in sculpture to social concerns in audio-visual media. Therefore, given this background and his studio training, it's hardly likely that he would have brought an academic social science perspective to his video studies. The key issue, though, is whether he achieves and makes possible a kind of ethnographic understanding comparable to that achieved by actual social scientists. The majority of the other attributes on Heider's grid all in some way relate to "ethnographic basis", and because Lange's studies perform well against them he makes up for in his practice what he may have lacked in his training. The question of "relation to printed materials" is also linked to second order attributes such as narration, and these pertain to the matter of the processing of research data, which is required to shift the studies to a higher level of analysis and synthesis. [22] If there is a pathway to this higher level in *Work Studies in Schools*, it comes from a mix of the following: the relationship between the reflexive discussion in the interview sessions and the records of the classroom lessons; the in-built comparative framework provided by the range of schools and subjects studied; and the implicit links between these studies and Lange's industrial work and related culture studies conducted inside and outside factories at similar times and places. However, it is up to the viewer to do the work required to get to this level.

In his prefatory statement to the catalogue of the Museum of Modern Art Oxford's exhibition of his *Work Studies in Schools*, Lange writes: "there is no word for art in the Polynesian language, and the Polynesians attempt to do everything as creatively as they can"; he goes on to suggest that "creativity in schools is not necessarily confined to the art class"; and, further on, he adds, "it might help to recreate involvement and creativity within manual work or build non-object recreational expression". [23] These statements –issued as a result of Lange's ongoing project of trying to map the meaning-making impulses underpinning various classroom "performances" by means of his own "performances" as a videographer – might best be understood in the terms formulated

22   The difficulty here is that Lange, as Guy Brett states, sacrificed "the power to synthesise". Guy Brett 'Introduction' in *Work Studies in Schools*, Museum of Modern Art Oxford, 1977, p. 3.

23   Lange, op.cit., p. 18.

Exacting Reproduction: Darcy Lange's *Work Studies in Schools*

by Paul Willis in a theoretical text published more than 20 years after the first edition of *Learning to Labour*. At the beginning of his book, *The Ethnographic Imagination*, Willis asks a key question: "… what are the consequences of viewing everyday relations as if they contained a creativity of the same order as that held to be self-evidently part of what we call the arts?" And, shortly after, he asserts, "meaning-making is not an internal quest … Meaning-making can be considered a work process involving its own kind of labour and expressive outcomes issuing into some kind of inter-subjective space". [24]

The first chapter of Willis's book, titled 'Life as Art', begins with an epigraphic quotation from the appendix to *Learning to Labour*, a comment from 'Joey' about his and the other lads' "own sort of art form". Willis glosses Joey's comment as follows: "Joey offers no finished poems. His poems are situated, performative and embodied in and through his whole social life and activity at school." [25] In light of this claim, we might ask what forms of creativity do Lange's school videotapes reveal? In all instances, the classroom sequences are to a large degree teacher-centred, not by virtue of the visuals, which, as Guy Brett notes, are delivered from "no special vantage-point" and are ruminative, [26] but by means of the soundtrack, which directs viewer-attention through the teachers' continuous monologues. The teacher interviews, conducted subsequent to the lesson, enable individual teachers to exchange a formal voice of pedagogic authority for an informal voice of dialogic reflection. Thus, this method delivers a more rounded picture of teacher practice, which is the principal form of work studied by the videotapes. Direct access to the voices of the pupils is limited to the post-viewing discussion sessions with selected groups. But, even then, the classroom teacher is still present. In relation to this schema, Guy Brett suggests, "there's no reason it couldn't be extended further." [27] It seems to me that the direction in which these studies could have been extended would have involved amplifying the voices of pupils, which remain relatively muted and constrained in the finished studies. But to do this, Lange, like Willis, would have had to establish spaces of interaction and rapport outside formal learning situations, which is what he wished to do. [28] If he had been able to do so, he might have shown something of what Willis refers to as "… the long history of antagonism and dependency between bodily and abstract forms of knowing, between the mental and the manual played out in cultural and everyday arenas". [29]

24 Paul Willis, *The Ethnographic Imagination*, Cambridge: Polity Press, 2000, p. xiv.

25 Ibid, pp. 3–4.

26 Brett, op.cit., p. 4. Lange's camera frequently wanders away from the teacher and the class, to take in details of the classroom setting. A particularly striking instance of this practice can be found in the study of Tony Morgan's art class at Banbury School, Oxfordshire. Here I would note an affinity with the camera style of Andy Warhol, of whose films Wayne Kostenbaum has written: "… the stationary camera is his trademark. (In his other films, when the camera budges, it erratically disregards the action, it digresses, ignores the star …)". *Andy Warhol*, London: Phoenix, 2001, p. 62.

27 Brett, op.cit., p. 4.

28 It is clear from a letter and a grant application amongst Lange's papers that he intended to extend the existing school studies beyond the classroom and into the informal settings of teachers' and pupils' homes; he also envisaged conducting interviews with "outside people of special interest in the subject". He intended to present the whole schools project in the 1977 *documenta*. However, he did not receive sufficient funding to realise the project in this form. Only his application to the Arts Council of Great Britain for a 16mm film grant was successful.

29 Willis, (2000) op.cit., p. 31.

Structural System of the Oxfordshire Project

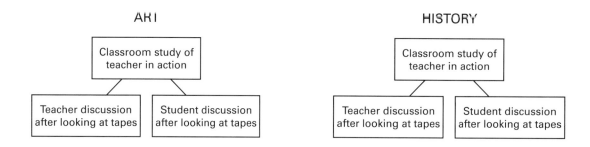

ART

Classroom study of
teacher in action

Teacher discussion
after looking at tapes

Student discussion
after looking at tapes

HISTORY

Classroom study of
teacher in action

Teacher discussion
after looking at tapes

Student discussion
after looking at tapes

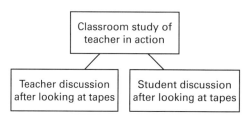

SCIENCE

Classroom study of
teacher in action

Teacher discussion
after looking at tapes

Student discussion
after looking at tapes

Banbury School
(Public school)
Ruskin Road, Banbury

Tony Morgan
Art teacher
Fifth Year CSE Group

Peter Garwood
History teacher
Fifth Year O Level

Julia Swift
Biology teacher
Fifth Year O Level

Cheney Upper School
(Public school)
Gypsy lane, Headington

Eric Spencer
Art teacher
Fifth Form

Chris Wright
History teacher
Fourth Form

Tom Bailey
Chemistry teacher
Form 3B

St. Mary's School
(Private school)
Newbury Street, Wantage

Mrs. Schalgosky
Art teacher
Upper Third

Mrs. D. Webb
History teacher
Upper Sixth

Miss H. Astani
Chemistry teacher
Upper Fifth

Radley College
(Private school)
Near Abingdon, Oxford

Charles Mussett
Art teacher
Shell Remove Option

Gerald Howatt
History teacher
First Year Sixth

Michael Lewis,
Duck Usherwood, Guy Waller
Chemistry teachers
First Year Sixth

However, it is clear from Lange's list of guidelines that his main focus is on teachers and the practice of classroom teaching, as both a form of work and a subtle disseminator of "middle class academic aspirations". [30] The number and variety of schools studied and the combination of observational and interview-based sequences, all conducted by means of the strategy of the long take, enabled Lange to compile a comprehensive and systematic profile of classroom pedagogy in the UK of the 1970s. In a manner analogous to conceptual art's embrace of the artless document over the crafted representation, Lange replaced the social scientist's processed field notes with audio-visual diaries of his classroom experiences. In doing so he adopted what David MacDougall calls an "unprivileged camera style", which avoids "singling out dramatic subjects for attention", but rather opens "the film to a kind of anti-subject matter" that deals with "apparently inconsequential events that were more like what one would witness in ordinary experience than choose as film subjects". [31] The enterprise as a whole was anchored by a grid, a systematic 'structural system' – derived, perhaps, from Lange's background in geometric sculptural construction – that enabled its individual parts to be correlated with each other and with their equally systematic cousins in the wider world of work. When these studies were first exhibited, Guy Brett stated: "It is hard to say what final form this accumulation of material could take [for] ... nobody knows quite how to categorise this kind of work." [32] The 'accumulation of material' that constitutes Lange's oeuvre now resides in the New Zealand Film Archive but the question of its 'final form' remains as unresolved now as it did then. However, given that Lange adhered consistently to a particularly rigorous form of process art and regarded these studies as a form of ongoing research, perhaps we should accept his work as a kind of video in perpetual motion, never finished only stopped for pragmatic reasons.

30 Lange, op.cit., p. 18.

31 David MacDougall, 'Unprivileged Camera Style' in *Transcultural Cinema*, Princeton: Princeton University Press, 1998, p. 200.

32 Brett, op.cit., p. 3.

Studies of Teaching in Four Oxfordshire Schools, UK, 1977

Studies of Teaching in Four Oxfordshire Schools, UK, 1977

Eric Spencer, art class, Cheney Upper School.

Studies of Teaching in Four Oxfordshire Schools, UK, 1977

Peter Garwood, history class, Banbury School.

Studies of Teaching in Four Oxfordshire Schools, UK, 1977

Miss H. Astani, chemistry class, Upper Fifth, St. Mary's School.

*Studies of Teaching in Four Oxfordshire
Schools, UK*, 1977

Miss H. Astani and students viewing and
discussing the recording.

Studies of Teaching in Four Oxfordshire Schools, UK, 1977

Chris Wright, history class, Cheney Upper School.

Chris Wright viewing the recording.

*Studies of Teaching in Four Oxfordshire
Schools, UK*, 1977

Charles Mussett, art class, Radley College.

Charles Mussett viewing the recording.

*Studies of Teaching in Four Oxfordshire
Schools, UK*, 1977

Tom Bailey, chemistry class, Cheney
Upper School.

Tom Bailey with students viewing
the recording.

Darcy Lange:
Māori Land Project –
Working in Fragments [1]

John Miller & Geraldene Peters

After completing the series *Work Studies in Schools* conducted
in England, Lange returned to New Zealand [2] during the winter
of 1977, and by June of that year had begun the bracket of work
that came to be known as *Māori Land Project*, [3] work that was to
continue through to the documentary *Lack of Hope – Co-op [sic] a
New Future* (1986–7). [4]

The work from the 1970s is a collection of film and video
footage that deals with Māori governance of the Ngatihine [5]
land block near Kawakawa, Tai Tokerau (Northland) and the
Takaparawha (Bastion Point) [6] reclamation of land from the Crown
in Auckland. *Lack of Hope* is in many respects a continuation
of that work. Indeed, in some instances, Lange revisits people
and regions he had worked with in the earlier footage, such as
David Goldsmith and Matiu Tarawa. These were symptomatic of
ongoing relationships that Lange sustained across the 1970s and
1980s. Although Lange could be considered as an 'outsider' in this
area of his work, he was not unfamiliar with Māori perspectives
during the early stages of his lifetime. [7] His family in Urenui, north
Taranaki worked closely with the local Ngati Mutunga community,
and Lange himself had close friendships with local people such
as 'Uncle' Ra Raumati, and later, Te Miringa Hohaia of Parihaka.
Other instances of sustained production relationships included
collaborative work with documentary photographers John Miller
and Ian Macdonald.

Land Alienation in the 1970s
The first phase of *Māori Land Project* was shot in New Zealand
during the late 1970s. Parts were then edited in the Netherlands
during 1978, culminating in exhibitions in the Netherlands and
Belgium in 1980. Lange was concerned with two distinctive case
studies of land alienation and Māori resistance to the dynamics of
colonialism that each case deployed – the Bastion Point occupation

1   Lange's long time friend and
collaborator John Miller has played a
crucial role in the process of identifying
archival materials. Although the
procedure of historicising through
Miller's recollections, diaries, letters,
meeting notes and telephone logs is
a contingent one, nonetheless it is
valuable for the coherency it lends to
this body of Lange's work.

2   In the interests of periodising work
produced for *Māori Land Project*, 'New
Zealand' rather than 'Aotearoa/New
Zealand' has been chosen as a term of
reference. For present-day purposes,
the term also carries with it an implied
relationship to Aotearoa.

3   Lange and others have given various
names to the body of work, for example,
'the Māori Land Video', 'the Aotearoa
Land Pains project', the Māori social,
cultural and land project. The name
'Māori Land Project' was the title given
to the Van Abbemuseum exhibition and
generally captures the range of work
associated with this topic.

4   Among the fragments of work from this
late 1970s period, there is one strand
that fits awkwardly with most of the
other *Māori Land Project* themes. It is
footage of a class run by teacher, David
Goldsmith, at Manutahi Primary School
near Ruatoria on the East Cape, and of
other classes and kapa haka activities
in Ruatoria. Filmed in the observational
style of the *Work Studies in Schools*,
Lange is thought to have shot this
material on a trip to the East Cape soon
after arriving back in New Zealand in
1978. It's tempting to speculate about
Lange's intention to continue with
school studies in New Zealand however,
the body of *Māori Land Project* material
indicates that his attention was drawn
elsewhere.

5   At the time of the dispute, the Ngatihine
Block Action Committee, publications
and media reports carried the spelling
Ngatihine. Presently the tribe self-
identifies as Ngati Hine although the
other form is still frequently used.

6   The Māori name for the land occupied
by Bastion Point is Takaparawhau. At
the time of the occupation, the land was
known as Takaparawha, the difference
has subsequently been attributed to
a misspelling: Sharon Hawke, (ed.)
Takaparawhau: The People's Story,
Moko Productions, Orakei, 1998.

7   See screening flyer: *Video Analysis
– Māori Land Issue*, Montevideo,
Amsterdam, 27 March to 6 April 1978.

and the work of the Ngatihine Block Action Committee (NBAC). These were two of many cases that pitched Māori against the Crown during the 1970s as a consequence of land alienation practices enabled through 19th century legislation such as the 1882 Ōrakei Native Reserve Act, as well as the Māori Affairs Act 1953 and its 1967 amendment. [8]

The Bastion Point occupation, or Takaparawha reclamation, was a high profile direct action occupation undertaken to prevent the permanent alienation of tribal ancestral land by a private subdivision. Ngati Whatua o Ōrakei (the Takaparawha iwi) had signalled a desire to reclaim that land as a part of the tribe's settlement process with the Crown subsequent to the establishment of the Waitangi Tribunal. [9] The Ngatihine case involved a prolonged Māori Land Court argument over the implementation of a large forestry scheme within the Ngatihine rohe (tribal area) in central Northland and the extent to which the land's owners had control over the leasing of it. [10] Common to both cases were the political and philosophical differences between Pakeha's desires to harness land for capital gain (land as commodity – the lure of prime residential real estate and industrial forestry) and Māori's desire for self-determination over decisions about the control and use of land (as taonga, or treasure). Ngatihine won their case in the Supreme Court in 1978, whereas Ngati Whatua were not able to gain settlement until the Ōrakei Report and Act of 1991.

The Takaparawha and Ngatihine footage was shot in 1977 with colour video equipment borrowed from the Auckland City Art Gallery with the help of Ian Macdonald, then an exhibitions officer at the gallery. [11] Much of the Ngatihine footage was the outcome of collaboration by Lange and Ngapuhi land rights activist John Miller. Similarly, a quality of intimacy suggests that the Bastion Point footage prior to editing could be understood as the outcome of a collaborative relationship between Lange and Joe Hawke, a leader and key spokesperson for the Bastion Point occupation. Virginia Shaw and Māori language campaigner Dun Mihaka conduct shopping centre vox pop in the culturally disparate suburbs of Otara and Browns Bay, in an attempt to gather a range of responses to the Bastion Point occupation. John Miller is filmed at Kaikou and Matawaia Marae (the Ngatihine heartland) in discussion with local farmers and fellow NBAC members Motatau Shortland, Moses Peihopa and others, then in

8   The latter since replaced by the Te Ture Whenua Act of 1993.

9   The Waitangi Tribunal was established in 1975 as a permanent government commission of inquiry. It is charged with making recommendations on claims brought by Māori relating to actions or omissions of the Crown that breach the promises made in the Treaty of Waitangi. The Treaty was signed in 1840 by the British colonial government and Māori tribal representatives. Although not a constitution, it has status as a foundational document for the nation of Aotearoa New Zealand. It was an agreement that consolidated British influence and contributed to the formation of legal and parliamentary structures of governance.

10   This reflected the ethos of the times that multiple Māori land ownership impeded the productive use of land.

11   The format was ¾ inch low-band U-matic shot on a Sony DXC-1600 Trinicon Tube hand-held colour camera. The unit included a VO-3800 20 minute cassette portapack and power unit, and VO-2630 VCR 60 minute cassette recording deck (mains powered). Sound was recorded through a Sennheiser shotgun microphone and a pair of Sony ECM 66B lavaliers.

later discussions with Mihaka and fellow land rights campaigner Matiu Tarawa. There is also full coverage of an NBAC meeting in Otara, including supporters Sandra Lee and David Williams, and a Māori Land Court meeting in Kawakawa. Other interviews were also included to give context to the social consequences of land alienation. For example, Dun Mihaka is filmed interviewing Jim and Mere Ransfield and their extended whanau (family) about the community house that they were running in Ponsonby for 'at risk' young people. [12] Expressions of frustration and a sense of powerlessness at the process of alienation were common to all of the interviews with Māori participants.

Two interviews were shot providing trenchant criticism of the government processes. Taura Eruera, one of the founders of Nga Tamatoa (young warriors) was interviewed earlier in 1977 offering a highly critical interpretation of the processes of colonialism. John Miller spoke on behalf of the NBAC about what he characterised as a 'forestry land grab' taking place on many North Island Māori land blocks. Their perspectives can be juxtaposed with two key interviews with Members of Parliament filmed during 1978 – Minister of Māori Affairs, Duncan MacIntyre of the National Party and Opposition spokesperson (and former Minister of Māori Affairs) Matiu Rata of the Labour Party. MacIntyre's discourse supports the Government line (which, despite the sympathies of some, did not support Māori grievances) and Rata's response, although not as vehement as that of Eruera or Miller, locates him as a figure in the process of moving away from Labour's moderate stance on Māori Land issues to establish the Mana Motuhake (Māori self-determination) Party in 1979. MacIntyre and Rata were interviewed respectively by current affairs journalists Catherine Judd and Bill Ralston. [13] Interestingly, both interviewers use the same question lines for each interviewee which suggests that Lange intended the interviews to provide some kind of bridging discourse, linking different elements of the footage shot in 1977. This is corroborated by the fact that although the footage was never edited into any finished documentary until 1979, Lange's negotiations with TV1, TV2 and Dutch television indicated that he did intend a television narrative outcome for the material as early as 1978.

The two Members of Parliament were also presenting opposing perspectives which may have had a dialectical function. [14] Obviously, they were expressing different party-political lines about the problem of Māori land. It's likely that Lange would have been

12 Importantly, the urbanisation of Māori was a contributing factor to Māori experiences of disenfranchisement. This was a consequence of post-war industrial growth in towns and cities which increased markedly during the 1960s through government relocation policies. Paul Meredith 'Urban Māori' in *Te Ara – the Encyclopedia of New Zealand*, updated 20 September, 2007, (www.teara.govt.nz/newzealanders/maorinewzealanders/urbanmaori/en).

13 During this time, Virginia Shaw, a close friend of Lange's, had begun working as a current affairs journalist for television and was able to draw in the assistance of people such as Ralston. Lange consistently struggled to make ends meet financially, hence production methods for the project were based on ad hoc voluntary assistance from friends, fellow artists and film-makers. Accordingly, the camera operator for the film version of the MacIntyre interview was left-wing film-maker Alister Barry who also assisted Lange with distribution for *Lack of Hope*.

14 Lange's experience with the social arts milieu in the UK of the 1960s and 1970s and his interest in socialist philosophy would suggest that he had an awareness of the function of dialectical relationships through art forms. Certainly, this was evident in his video art/television/political documentary collaboration with René Coelho, Leonard Henny and the Victor Jara Collective in Amsterdam who were explicitly interested in the dialectical juxtaposition of ideas and media. See *Video Analysis – Māori Land Issue,* Montevideo, Amsterdam, 27 March to 6 April 1978.

aware of the possibilities of commenting ironically on processes of neo-colonialism by positioning MacIntyre against the whare tūpuna (ancestral house) backdrop of Parliament's Māori Affairs committee rooms and Rata against the backdrop of a series of Gottfried Lindauer [15] paintings at the Auckland City Art Gallery. [16] The MacIntyre interview was shot in both 16mm film and video, which may have been intended as commentary on the different media. Certainly, as a video artist of the 1970s, Lange would have been alert to questions of the dialectical relationship between film and video form. [17]

Travelling by himself in Kawerau during 1977, Lange interviewed Tim Horopapera, a Tasman Pulp and Paper mill worker and unionist. Horopapera was critical of the way in which ancestral land was being taken over by forestry companies with little recompense for the traditional owners. This footage is also intriguing for its experimentation with the video apparatus and filming techniques. The interview is constructed through several takes with a variation in the shot sizes that frame Horopapera. It's a sense of video process that recalls Lange's earlier concerns with constructions of a reaction in the *Work Studies in Schools* series.

Takaparawha/Bastion Point

The occupation of Bastion Point had been under way several months by the time Lange arrived back in New Zealand. [18] The lack of any winter footage, corroborated by Joe Hawke's commentary in the video, suggested that Lange did not begin filming until the later months of 1977. [19] The intimacy of Lange's footage and his characteristic use of long, reflective takes distinguishes his material from news reportage and the combination of montage energy and expressive soundtrack in *Bastion Point Day 507*. [20] Lange's camera captures everyday life occurrences at the site of occupation – human interactions, the layout of the encampment and the Takaparawha landscape. Filmed in observational style and in different settings (Takaparawha, the Savage memorial, Maungawhau (Mt Eden), Paritai Drive and Queen Street), Joe Hawke reflects on the tribal, political, legal and historical context of the occupation. There are discussions with whanau and other activists over breakfast and late at night in the wharenui (meeting house), Arohanui. The intimacy of the footage suggests that, at least at the stage of filming, a relationship of trust was established between Lange and Joe Hawke.

15 Gottfried or Bohumir Lindauer (5 January 1839 to 13 June 1926) was a New Zealand artist of Czech descent famous for his portraits of prominent Māori chiefs. His purpose in painting these portraits was to maintain a record of what was then perceived to be a dying race of people.

16 Although the Māori Affairs committee room was also known to be a convenient Parliamentary venue for sit-down interviews with visiting politicians and dignitaries.

17 Certainly, this was consistent with his parallel use of video and film (and some photography) in earlier studies such as *A Documentation of Calverton and Pleasley Coal Mining Communities, Nottingham* (1973) and *A Documentation of Bradford WorkingLife* (1974), even his unfinished or failed parallel film project to his *Work Studies in Schools, Film Studies in Comprehensive and Grammar Schools* (1976–7). By the 1980s this structural interest in the media seems to have faded away. Perhaps because of Lange's more concentrated interest in the informational content of what he was recording, and because the video medium was more cost-effective and easier to use.

18 The occupation lasted 506 days from 5 January, 1977 to 25 May, 1978.

19 Lange filmed one sequence with Joe Hawke at Bastion Point around 20 October, 1977, three weeks after the death of Joanne Hawke in a fire in the occupation camp on 28 September. This timing is mentioned in Joe's monologue to camera.

20 *Bastion Point Day 507* (1980) a documentary produced through the collective efforts of Merata Mita, Leon Narbey and Gerd Pohlmann, focused on the final days leading up to the eviction of protestors from Takaparawha. It is significant among both Māori and Pakeha communities as a visual record of the activity of tūpuna (elders, ancestors) and key participants in the occupation, as well as in terms of political film-making practices in this country. Interestingly, footage of the eviction shot by an unknown film-maker appeared in both *Bastion Point Day 507* and Lange's Bastion Point film.

Lange left New Zealand in December travelling through North America, London and the Netherlands, returning to New Zealand during July of 1978. Before leaving, he approached TV1 and the Queen Elizabeth II Arts Council for funding to support the editing and post-production of the footage and continued those discussions through letters and the intercessions of friends while overseas. Both organisations wanted to see more detailed indications of Lange's intentions for the footage before committing funds. Television wanted to see a rough cut and the Arts Council offered to sponsor a one-way airfare to enable Lange's return to New Zealand: other funds would be contingent on the progress of the work. With a belief that Bastion Point issues required more international exposure, Lange also tried North American sources such as the National Endowment for the Humanities and the CBS television producers of *60 Minutes*, but without success. He elicited the support of friends such as Phil Dadson and Virginia Shaw to continue contact with the Arts Council, media agencies and potential editors on his behalf. The need for an editor seemed crucial to Lange, at various stages he was trying to persuade John Miller and Phil Dadson to take on the role. Dadson, Shaw and the Queen Elizabeth II Arts Council were part of a small chorus of people during early 1978 urging Lange to return from overseas and edit the film in New Zealand. There were compelling reasons for doing so – firstly, to justify state funds supporting post-production and secondly, so that Lange would be able to maintain a close connection with the issues and the people he filmed. This second reason hints at the tension that existed between the vision of the individual artist, and Lange's ethical obligations to the communities he was working with. It had been very difficult to find someone in Europe of Māori descent with sufficient knowledge of tikanga Māori (Māori culture) who could write a script or edit the footage.

The interviews with Rata and MacIntyre were the only indicators of a desire to introduce narrative coherency into the proposed work. These were not shot until after Lange's return in July of 1978, having secured a firm indication of interest in a 20 minute television documentary from NOS/Panoramiek in the Netherlands. This is consistent with Lange's statements, in a letter to Joe Hawke and in an interview for the *Māori Land Project* museum catalogue, that his initial intention was always to make a series of poetic video recordings and that the television programme was an afterthought, intended to assist Māori with the international articulation of land alienation struggles. He continued to pursue local television options and TV2 also showed interest in the material. Lange showed footage to Tainui representatives and received a mixed response largely due to the political allegiances of those consulted. Some preferred to see cultural events rather than land alienation issues discussed on television. Nonetheless, TV2 was interested in pursuing the options with Tainui support. For reasons unknown, the project never eventuated. Lange's interest in the documentary possibilities of his footage has to be understood in terms of his awareness of significant documentaries exploring New Zealand and the Māori Renaissance produced by his friends and contemporaries. [21] Phil Dadson, Leon Narbey and Geoff Steven had made *Te Matakite o Aotearoa/The Māori Land March* in 1975 for South Pacific Television, Chris Strewe had made *Waitangi: The Story of A Treaty and its Inheritors* in 1977 as both his graduate work for the Berlin Film School and for German television, and Barry Barclay had directed the *Tangata Whenua* television series in 1974 – fragments of all three works appear in the film that Lange edited for exhibition. [22]

Auckland City Art Gallery

Lange left the country again between late September and late November for an invitation by Dan Graham to lecture at NSCAD University, Halifax, Canada in October and at the Academy of Fine Arts, Design and Architecture (AKI) in Enschede, the Netherlands in November. Before leaving, plans were well underway to organise a photographic and video exhibition at the Auckland City Art Gallery around the theme of Māori land alienation. This had its genesis in an invitation sent to Lange in 1977 to participate in the *Vanguard* exhibition series and through Lange's communications with the gallery directorship during the first half of 1978. Indigenous activist, Colin Clark, of the Ōrakei Māori Action Committee, was a principal supporter and had been travelling through the country during the year consulting with iwi and collating exhibits and information about taonga – without any financial support. Lange and Clark visited the far north, filming the people of Clark's rohe (district) of Te Aupōuri and Te Rarawa living in rural tent encampments and on marae. By this stage, Lange had returned the video equipment to the Auckland City Art Gallery so

21 'The Māori Renaissance' describes a period since the late 1960s until the present day, where Māori have become much more proactive in advancing indigenous self-determination through historic Treaty land claims, language and educational reforms and strengthening the management of commercial enterprises connected with land and marine resources. This has been tied to an increased involvement in the production of indigenous arts and news media.

22 This video was made in conjunction with the exhibition of Lange's *Māori Land Project* at the Internationaal Cultureel Centrum (ICC), Antwerp and Montevideo/TBA, in Amsterdam, the Netherlands. It was produced by Leonard Henny from Werkgroep Internationale Solidariteit (WIS), a centre dedicated to the research of media and its uses as political tool. As it was produced in the Netherlands for Dutch audiences, this documentary contains introductory information about Aotearoa New Zealand as well as a timeline of Bastion Point events. The credits specify: camera editing and concept: Darcy Lange; production assistance: Leonard Henny WIS; ICC; Montevideo/TBA; René Coelho, Studio IM Utrecht, NZArts Council, Auckland City Art Gallery, NZ.

all of the footage was shot mute on a Bolex film camera – some of
which appears in Lange's exhibition documentary. [23] By September
of 1978, the plans for a 1979 exhibition were in disarray with the
gallery's recommendation to transfer the exhibition to Outreach, a
community arts centre in Ponsonby. There was disbelief and anger
on the part of documentary's proponents, and the negotiations
that ensued from the resulting fallout involved Māori community
leaders, gallery management, the Race Relations Conciliator and
the Queen Elizabeth II Arts Council. The exhibition was never
realised. Lange returned to New Zealand in late November and left
again for the Netherlands in mid-February 1979.

The Netherlands

During the course of his visits to the Netherlands, Lange
had established a relationship with René Coelho, director of
Montevideo/TBA, then a newly established video art gallery.
Coelho had been a television producer and arranged for Lange
to produce the 25 minute documentary for public broadcaster,
NOS Television. Coelho introduced him to sociologist/visual
anthropologist Leonard Henny of the Centre for International
Media Research in Utrecht. Henny, a film-maker as well as an
academic, was interested in the conjunction of film and video with
'action research' methodologies informed by the work of theorist-
practitioner Paolo Freire among others. He worked together with a
revolutionary film-makers cooperative from Guyana, the Victor Jara
Collective based in Amsterdam. The collective had just completed
a documentary critiquing British neo-colonialism and state
repression in Guyana and had been employed by the University of
Utrecht to teach film production methods.

    After some discussion, Lange and the collective agreed to
work together on editing the *Māori Land Project* footage gathered
thus far. There was a fit between the collective's desire to work in
solidarity with another culture struggling against neo-colonialist
pressures and Lange's need for empathetic editing assistance. A
decision was made to produce three projects – a 25 minute piece
for NOS produced by Coelho, two versions of a 20 minute piece
for a university research project by Henny and the Victor Jara
Collective, and a much longer piece directed by Lange. [24] Māori
involvement with the editing processes was considered crucial
and Lange and Henny undertook to raise funds to transport a
Māori representative to Amsterdam in order to supervise the

23 See note 20.

24 Two versions of Lange's documentary
exist in the archives, one is 300
minutes long and the other is 150
minutes. The films edited for Henny's
university research project were
designed to test the political efficacy
and pedagogical function of films
made to educate people about issues
for people in developing companies.
A systematic audience research
project was designed drawing from
responses in schools, church groups
and 'third-world' solidarity groups
within the Netherlands. The two
versions of the Bastion Point film
were edited distinctively to represent
a 'point of view' and a balanced
perspective of the issues (one included
commentary by Māori, the other only
featured interviews with Pakeha).
The responses of school children to
each version were then compared to
determine the kind of 'consciousness
raising' that each generated. See
Leonard Henny, *Raising Consciousness
Through Film: Audio-Visual Media and
International Development Education*,
Sociological Institute, University of
Utrecht, Netherlands, 1980.

edits. Correspondence suggests that Joe Hawke was prepared to go and Lange had been assured of airfare costs from the Van Abbemuseum, however funding apparently fell through at the last minute. The Victor Jara Collective was particularly sensitive to the need for participant involvement in the editing and both they and Henny expressed concern at the limitations of working without sustained direct contact with Māori involved in the struggle. Vivienne Wreidjrenger, a young Dutch-Māori woman (who had joined the Bastion Point occupation as a cousin to the Hawke family) was visiting Amsterdam and sat in on parts of the edit, but her input was limited by a lack of knowledge about specific incidents. Henny, Lange and the Victor Jara Collective put effort into maintaining correspondence with John Miller, who transmitted their concerns to others who were participating in the documentary. Although well intentioned, there were obvious limitations to consultation over the edit by airmail.

Lange's letters to Miller and Hawke indicated that at some stage the relationship between Lange and Hawke had broken down, ostensibly over the belief that through the documentary project, Lange had sold the Bastion Point footage to Dutch television. Lange denies this and his letters consistently suggest that he was convinced of the beneficial value of bringing the Māori land issues to world attention through the video projects, that his motivation was to "help" Māori. Certainly, Lange's near-impoverished financial circumstances suggest he never benefited financially from his work. Correspondence also suggests that Hawke consistently voiced his concerns that the documentary be produced with due care for the complexity of the issues, particularly in relation to Takaparawha/Bastion Point. Although it's clear that Lange tried everything within his power to find the money to bring a Māori consultant to Amsterdam, ultimately there was no mandated representative participating in the production of the documentary and other films. From today's standpoint, the lack of informed consultation at the crucial editing stage and the decision to proceed with the films despite this, denied Ngati Whatua o Ōrakei the opportunity for self-determination through visual representation – although unintentional, this was effectively another form of colonisation.

As an indication of redress, Henny attempted to extend the work of the video/film projects by facilitating connections between Māori and other indigenous peoples seeking recognition of indigenous struggle within international legislative assemblies such as the United Nations, which in turn would lead to increased pressure on national governments to address indigenous rights. He successfully sought funds for a Māori representative to attend the Fourth Russell Tribunal for the Rights of the Indians of the Amerikas held in Rotterdam at the end of November 1980. Colin Clark was able to represent the case for understanding the alienation of Māori from ancestral lands as a violation of human rights, and extensive video coverage of those hearings is among the *Māori Land Project* tapes.

Working in the Netherlands also gave Lange the opportunity to, at least partially, realise the museum exhibition that never eventuated in New Zealand. In the early months of 1980, the exhibition was hosted at the Stedlijk Van Abbemuseum in Eindhoven, the Netherlands and then travelled to the Internationaal Cultureel Centrum in Antwerp, Belgium. The exhibition consisted of the three video/film projects, slides photographed by Lange, printed documentation including books, newspaper and magazine articles, excerpts from other documentaries used in the films and a catalogue that included interviews, essays and transcripts contextualising the exhibition and its content. [25] In 1979, Lange had corresponded with Ian Murray and Peggy Gale (director of A Space in Toronto), Jo-Anne Birnie Danzker (Vancouver Art Gallery curator) and Brian Dyson (Alberta College of Art Gallery curator) about touring the exhibition to Canada. However, this never eventuated, possibly because of the lack of European equipment in Canada.

Subsequent to the Russell Tribunal and his work with Henny, Lange envisaged a larger participatory action video event known as the *Haka/Four Winds Project* involving screenings of the Bastion Point footage and audience interaction with those screenings, in conjunction with an international media workshop training indigenous peoples in media use and the archiving of audio-visual materials. One goal was to further Colin Clark's desire for a Pacific version of the Russell Tribunal, linking the local specificity of Takaparawha and other cases of land alienation with global indigenous struggle. It was also seen as a means of developing the work Clark had already produced for the Auckland City Art Gallery exhibition that never eventuated. John Miller noted that an initial meeting was held to discuss these possibilities, but the project did not advance any further.

25 See exhibition catalogue *Darcy Lange: Māori Land Project*, Stedelijk Van Abbemuseum, Eindhoven, 11 January to 10 February 1980. Internationaal Cultureel Centrum, Antwerpen, 29 March to 27 April 1980.

Lack of Hope

During January of 1984, Lange returned to settle in New Zealand for good together with his partner Maria Snijders and a child, Darcy Junior. 1984 was also the year that the Fourth Labour Government came to power laying the groundwork for a period of economic restructuring that took many people by surprise and had tragic outcomes for some. Importantly for the concerns Lange addressed in *Lack of Hope*, the neo-liberal reforms introduced unemployment on a scale never seen before in New Zealand. [26]

Lange's socialist-humanism informed his perspective that Māori communal support structures were a way forward to solve some of the issues facing people whose ways of living had been destroyed through the new right economic reforms in the process of being established at this time. The key argument of this documentary is that unemployment is a Pakeha problem, but one that can potentially be solved through Māori systems of communal work practices such as the arts activities of the Tūhoe Trust Board and the self-sufficiency programmes of the Whanau-a-Apanui in the Bay of Plenty.

Lange, again with the assistance of Ian Macdonald, had successfully applied to the Queen Elizabeth ll Arts Council for funding to purchase a Video8 camera along with CRT monitor, mains power edit deck and controller. [27] The resulting documentary includes interviews and observations in Auckland, Taranaki and the East Coast with people from unemployed workers rights centres, unions, a horticultural initiative and regionally-based co-operatives concerned with building, metal work, woodwork and small-scale engineering projects. Lange's ad-hoc interview style and process of gathering material were similar to techniques used for the 1970s *Māori Land Project* material. Interview questions were informed by very little, if any, research or planning. Instead, interviewees would be filmed speaking spontaneously about their topics, often in a conversational style. Lange and Miller worked together closely on one particular section of the documentary and during September and October of 1986, the pair made a two-week road trip around the East Coast of the North Island with a Video8 camera to visit local communities and discuss issues of unemployment. The footage gathered had a particular, although not exclusive, focus on the significance of forestry industries within the region. Accordingly, contemplative landscape cutaways and pans of the forestry plantations became important stylistic features

26 The perspectives within *Lack of Hope* can be complemented by the documentary *In Our Own Time – Unemployed Respond to Unemployment*, (1988) made at around the same time by left-wing film-makers Andrea Bosshard, Shane Loader and Jeremy Royal. Its topic was the national organisation for unemployed people, Te Roopu Rawakore O Aotearoa.

27 The camera was the Sony CCD-V8AF camcorder in the newly introduced Video8 format. Miller constructed a small motorbike battery powerpack to extend the camera's running time.

of the documentary. Lange and Miller took turns with camera operation and the trip included Rotorua, Kawerau, Rūatoki, Taneatua, Waipiro and Whanarua Bays and Ruatoria.

In the Ureweras, Lange and Miller stayed on the summit of Taiarahia Mountain during the 'Nga Tamariki o te Kohu' (Children of the Mist) protest against plans to invite a local forestry company, Tasman Pulp and Paper, to plant the land in pine trees. Activists were in opposition to their trust board who wanted to lease the ancestral pa site to the company. Tame Iti and a local elder visited the encampment and are interviewed overlooking the Rūatoki valley. [28] In Taneatua, coverage included a local PEP scheme that involved the Tūhoe Training Assistance Programme running a music workshop for local musicians in the Taneatua Scout Hall. [29] A screen-printing workshop at the Tūhoe Skills Centre/Rūatoki School and flax weaving activities at a neighbouring marae are also included in this footage. The film-makers encountered an extension of the Ngatihine theme in Waipiro Bay with traditional Māori owners responding to the threat of Māori-leased land being taken over by forestry plantations. At Whanarua Bay, they videoed Hoani Park working in his garden as part of the Whanau-a-Apanui horticulture scheme using whanau land for subsistence as well as to grow and sell cash crops.

While visiting Hoani and Ra Park, Lange used the camera and CRT monitor to show footage shot in Rūatoki to the extended family group. He was to follow the same kind of travelling video process in Ruatoria, effectively communicating news of activity within the district to different community groups. Although the practice of travelling film or video for internal community or district use and for communication between community groups was not uncommon, new technological developments enabled a more immediate process of recording and viewing. This process had been intrinsic to his practices in Europe. This was exemplified formally through the *Work Studies in Schools* series, and informally when Lange showed his footage to the Bradford workers and the Spanish Farmers in Cantavieja, 1974. In the context of Aotearoa New Zealand, it may have also been an opportunity for Lange to follow up on plans established as early as 1978 to apply for Arts Council funding of a 'media van' equipped to travel between marae and other rural stations recording and screening material made for local communities.

28 Tame Iti (Tūhoe) was an original member of Nga Tamatoa. Since the 1970s, Iti has maintained a strong advocacy for indigenous rights through his community social work, specific protest actions and in recent years through his artwork. He was one of several people charged with offences under the Terrorism Suppression Act, during controversial police raids on the Ruatoki community in October, 2007. The Tūhoe people never signed the Treaty of Waitangi and were the last of the Māori tribes to submit to the control of government authority less than a century ago. They still maintain a strong sense of independence in upholding their traditions of language and culture.

29 The PEP (Project Employment Programmes) scheme was a government-run 'work for the dole (unemployment benefit)' programme. Also, Miller recalls that much to the delight of the trainees Lange, a skilled flamenco guitarist, demonstrated his own musical skills with an impromptu recital.

In Ruatoria, Lange and Miller recorded a significant hui (meeting) at Mangahanea Marae. Members of local communities met with officials from the Prime Minister's department, responding angrily to the Government's intentions to dis-establish all New Zealand Forestry Service (NZFS) activities on the East Coast – the region would suffer huge job losses. As a rural area, populated largely by Māori communities, Ruatoria relied heavily on work associated with the NZFS: people were employed to keep forestry roads in order, to staff the local telephone exchanges between forestry stations and to drive the service buses for the community and forestry employees. In effect, the rural economy was about to go to the wall. Lange and Miller recorded two hours of angry rhetoric where forestry workers threatened to burn down forests in protest and actor, Wi Kuki Ka, reprised his lines from the award-winning feature film *Ngati* (1986) to call for community control of local enterprises threatened with closure.

Consistent with a thematic focus on the erosion of community economic infrastructure, a side trip was taken to Tokomaru Bay to film the ruins of a local freezing works. Lange and Miller also contemplated continuing the journey to Hawke's Bay to interview freezing workers at the Whakatu freezing works in Hastings which had just been marked down for closure, but Lange was called home to attend pressing family matters. Miller observed that at times, Lange found it difficult to balance his aspirations for the documentary with the necessity of helping to provide for the family.

Conclusion

The excavation of *Māori Land Project* has been a process of recovering a narrative constructed through fragments of memory, footage, letters, diaries, etc. Even the edited material remains in fragments if we consider its at times inchoate nature. The project was one built on partially realised plans and prospects for bridging the conceptual and physical spaces of art work/gallery, documentary/public television, and community film – plans that were either never realised, or at least realised differently from how they were first conceived because of institutional politics, bureaucratic dysfunction and the metaphorical, and at times literal, difficulties Lange had finding a home. Certainly, the broken-ness of the project reflects Lange's experience of financial hardship and the failure of creative institutions within New Zealand to support his work through sustained employment and recognition. It is also broken in the sense of a Pakeha attempt to collaborate with Māori and articulate indigenous struggle within an international context. That said, the attendant translation failures had as much to do with the difficulties Lange had reconciling his socialist-informed ideals with the individualist inclinations of an artist as they had to do with ethnic difference.[30]

Importantly, the project is a sustained political piece if we consider the extent to which the themes of the late 1970s work are carried over to the *Lack of Hope* material. However, although consistent with Lange's earlier work in terms of demonstrating an interest in ethnicity, class, everyday life, and working processes in factories and rural environs this latter documentary sits more easily within the context of political documentary/community video than within a gallery space. This sense of disconnect has its corollary in attempts to historicise Lange's *Māori Land Project* – a methodology that in many ways moves against the grain of Lange's struggle to work with (or avoid) linear narrative coherence – providing a set of tensions that offers places of departure for further work.

30 Exhibition Catalogue, *Darcy Lange: Māori Land Project*, Stedelijk Van Abbemuseum Eindhoven 11 January to 10 February 1980. Internationaal Cultureel Centrum, Antwerpen 29 March to 27 April 1980, p. 33.

Works, 1977–88

Māori Land Project, 1977–80

'Fourth Russell Tribunal'
Colin Clark, Māori spokesman
for Aotearoa/New Zealand,
Rotterdam, 1980.

Māori Land Project, 1977–80

Duncan McIntyre interview (Minister of
the Māori Affairs, National Party).

Mata Rata interview (former Minister of
the Māori Affairs, Labour Party, at the
Auckland City Art Gallery).

Taura Eruera (Māori activist).

Ngatihine Block, 1977

John Miller discussing Māori territory on the North Island.

Bastion Point, 1977

Bastion Point, 1977

Māori Land Project, 1977–80

Darcy Lange with Motatau Shorthand
during the videotaping of the Ngatihine
Block in 1977, photograph by John Miller.

People of the World, 1983–4

Performance in the Netherlands.

Aire del Mar, 1988–94

Performance at City Art Gallery,
Wellington 1988.
Photograph by John Miller.

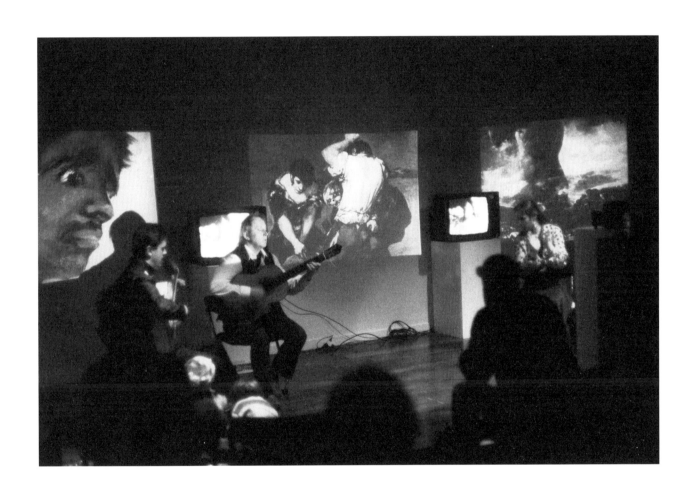

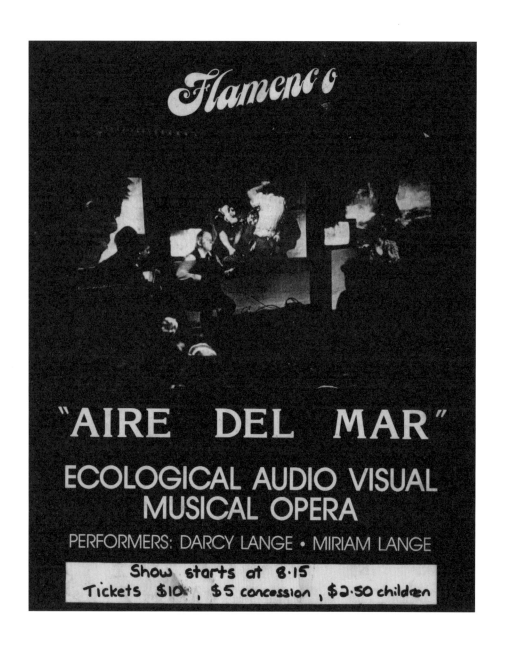

Poster for performance of *Aire del Mar.*

Antipodes: Darcy Lange, Work and Flamenco in the Image Chain of Production

Pedro G. Romero

Yo te estoy queriendo a ti,
Que yo te estoy queriendo a ti,
Que con la misma violencia
que lleva el ferrocarril.

(*I love you, I love you, with the same violence that drives a train*). Popular song, interpreted by Joselero de Morón as Soleares de la Sierra de Grazalema, in *Cantes Populares Españoles* by Francisco Rodríguez Marín, 1883, and *Colección de Cantes Flamencos* by Antonio Machado y Álvarez, 1947.

The lack of attention, and even the disdain which Marx [1] showed for the lumpenproletariat, that overflowing composite of social groups at the lower margins of the working classes, certainly would have hindered him from formulating a standpoint on consumer society, the absolute dominion of capital in postmodern, post-Fordian, post-industrial societies, or whatever one may choose to call them. The definition itself of the term lumpenproletariat is slippery enough, and the definitions applied to this social stratum are bound to elicit a wide range of adjectives, but little of real substance. It is interesting that Marx's own definition of the term, which appeared in 1845 in *German Ideology*, was closely linked to Hegel's notion of the 'Pöbel' (rabble or riff-raff), which isolated from the working class those elements in the proletariat – the beggars, thieves and prostitutes – deemed non-productive, and thus the lowest, least desirable and most dangerous of the social classes. In *Class Struggle in France*, he described this class as "gens sans feu et sans aveu" (people without hearth or home). However, for Marx, both classes, the proletariat and lumpenproletariat, had the following in common: they were 'free' and easily 'bought' or 'corruptible'. Thus, the lumpenproletariat was corrupted by this same capital and its asocial practices, which likewise situated them as outcasts or a non-class. In his *Letter to Cafiero*, one of the first translators of *Capital*, as recrimination for his siding with

1   Karl Marx, *La Ideología Alemana*, Grijalbo (ed.), Barcelona,1980; *La Lucha de Clases en Francia*, Espasa-Calpe (ed.), Madrid, 1992; *Escritos Sobre España*, Trotta (ed.), Barcelona, 1998; *El Capital*, Crítica (ed.), Barcelona, 1980; *Revolución en España*, Ariel (ed.), Barcelona, 1960.

Bakunin and his associates, Hegel describes the lumpen masses as follows: "it is the party of lowlifes and gypsies, only attracting the malcontent peasant masses, be they illuminated or esoteric, mystic or quite mad, or the mangy bootlickers, beggars and hitmen, who are inevitably as much an enemy of the proletariat as the Reaction". Interestingly enough, Engels or Pannekoek seem to link all these characteristics to southern Spain, a generalisation which might help to explain the prevalence of anarchist sympathies among Andalusian workers: in other words, the condition of the gypsy as a member of the non-class and a supporter of reaction. In his *Eighteenth Brumaire of Louis Bonaparte*, Marx again provides us with a definition of the lumpenproletariat:

> ... decayed roués; discharged soldiers, discharged jailbirds, escaped galley slaves, swindlers, mountebanks, pickpockets, tricksters, gamblers, pimps, brothel keepers, porters, literati, organ grinders, rag pickers, knife grinders, tinkers, beggars – in short, the whole indefinite, disintegrated mass, thrown hither and thither, which the French call *la bohème*.

It would seem obvious that without bohemian life, which for the French derives literally from connotations of gypsy life, aesthetic modernity cannot be understood. And flamenco is little more than the composite of music and dance expressions, a tool for survival and a way of life for one of these lumpenproletariat groups, the gypsies and 'agitanados' (those adapting a gypsy lifestyle) who have lived at the margins of the larger Andalusian cities since the mid-19th century.

It might therefore seem somewhat paradoxical that Darcy Lange, whose artwork is structured on images of work that directly stem from the material world formulated by Marx, should find his own vital counterpoint in flamenco, particularly in the world which Diego del Gastor had constructed from his guitar in Morón de la Frontera, Spain. In the episode devoted to Diego, part of the magnificent television series *Rito y Geografía del Cante Flamenco* [2] (*The Rituals and Geography of Flamenco Music*), Diego stated the following in response to questions posed by his students: "I have people [here] from all over, not only Americans, but even ...", he stutters over New Zealand without managing to pronounce it correctly, "... what's it called ... Japan ..." a student calls out, "even further away ... Australia," says another, "well, yes, even from there,

2 *Rito y Geografía del Cante Flamenco*, directed by Mario Gómez for TVE, episode devoted to Diego del Gastor, whose music was also used for the series soundtrack, aired in October 1972. Edition issued on DVD, by RTVE, Madrid, 2006.

Antipodes: Darcy Lange, Work and Flamenco in the Image Chain of Production

and also from here, these days". He could have been talking about Darcy Lange, or any other member of the international proletariat who had come to learn Diego's own style of guitar playing, and his way of life, and Lange would also pay his own tribute. Many of these acolytes were inspired by Donn E. Pohren's chronicle *A Way of Life*. [3] As Dan Graham observes: "In the 1970s, avant-garde rock and experimental music in New York occupied a position of marginalisation not dissimilar to that of flamenco". [4] Graham refers in particular to the Diego del Gastor myth which Lange had contributed to transmitting, since at the time flamenco had a tremendously important position in Andalusian society, and was permeated by a wide range of styles, from late pro-Franco popular songs to Communist music of protest, from flamenco pop for tourist consumption to the most underground forms of experimentalism, and which also considered Diego del Gastor's own brand of primitivism – somewhat paradoxically – part of its most highly prized folk roots.

Diego del Gastor, [5] who was from a gypsy background, was a fiercely independent and highly unique personality. He was not educated but he did have a rather thorough knowledge of García Lorca's poetry. His wisdom, however, shone through in other ways, most notably in his love for life. He learned from teachers such as Pepe Mesa not only his signature toque or guitar style but a sense of autonomy which he incorporated in his professional guitar playing. He played as he came to understand life. He would bring his dynamic rhythms wherever and to whomever he pleased, as a movable feast punctuated by mystic or meditative pauses. He never recorded a single album, yet his performances were appreciated by some of the most authentic flamenco singers of the time: Manolito de María, Juan Talega, Fernanda de Utrera, and even, polemically, the 'Pope' of the genre Antonio Mairena. Various circumstances in his life, including communal solidarity with his gypsy compatriots, enabled him to go on living this way, with minimal expense and maximum intensity.

With the signing of various bilateral agreements between the United States and the Franco dictatorship, a joint Spanish/ United States air base was established at Morón de la Frontera. Although operations there did not commence until the 1960s, works had been initiated and the town began reaping the benefits as early as 1953. The importance of this American base for the entire region is paradigmatic in all senses. [6] And, lest we forget,

3   Donn E. Pohren, *A Way of Life*, Society of Spanish Studies, New York, 1980.

4   Dan Graham, 'Darcy Lange: Work and Music', *New Observation*, No. 29, 1985.

5   Diego del Gastor's surname derives from his place of birth, El Gastor, a small town in the Sierra de Grazalema. A highly personal artist, he was the master of a somewhat rudimentary guitar technique, one which he used to extraordinary effect. His work – indebted as it was to the 19th century style purveyed by the Paco de Lucena school, as well as the falsetas (sets of melodic phrases) guitar virtuoso Andrés Segovia was recording at the time – resonated from the very musical depths of the town he would call his own, Morón de la Frontera. It was here that guitarists such as El Niño de Morón, Pepe Naranjo and Pepe Mesa had served as a chain for transmitting this particular guitar style. His family had made their fortune raising cattle and trading in fabrics. This gave him the freedom to learn the basics of singing and professional guitar playing. He avoided military service during the Spanish Civil War, or 'the war of the non-gypsies', as he later described it to Ángel Sody, through the standard gypsy practice of 'buying' exemption. In Morón de la Frontera, the Civil War lasted only a few weeks, however the repression imposed by the Fascists was enduring and severe. After the war, the family fortunes crumbled, and with his father's death, Diego took control of the household, imprinting his own style and understanding of life. The gypsies' marginalisation as a non-class enabled them to survive with some degree of ambiguity under the Franco regime. For Pohren, Diego had a basic affinity for military life and its predilection for order, while Ángel Sody, his other biographer, regarded him as an individualist and a rebel, without any defined political militancy, one who was always conscious of the suffering of the less fortunate. Ángel Sody de Rivas, *Diego del Gastor, El Eco de Unos Toques*, El Flamenco Vive, Madrid, 2004.

6   For example, the famous song 'La Macarena,' performed by Los del Río, which at one point served as a leitmotif for the Clinton presidential campaign, was little more than a rumba version of a children's song, also adapted as a marching theme for the U.S. marines. Thus, when dancing the 'Macarena' the Latino electorate was also hearing the undertones of a military exercise.

7   Serge Guilbaut, *De Cómo Nueva York Robó a París la Idea de Arte Moderno*, Editorial Tirant lo Blanc, Barcelona, 2007; Frances Stonor Saunders, *La Cía y la Guerra Fría Cultural*, debate, Barcelona, 2004; Jorge Luis Marzo, *Art Modern i Franquisme, Els Orígens Conservadors de l'Avantguarda i de la Política Artística a Espanya*, Fundació Espais, Gerona, 2007; Alfredo Grimaldos, *La CIA en España, Espionaje, Intrigas y Política al Servicio de Washington*, debate, Barcelona, 2006.

8   Tom Sorensen, known among flamenco musicians as Tomás de Utrera (Utrera is a small city near Morón de la Frontera), was an English instructor at the Cultural Center as well as a renowned flamenco guitarist and recording artist of some repute. He also undoubtedly served as a special informant to Miro Morville, then director of the center, who had his own ties to United States intelligence. Another interesting case is that of Moreen Silver, also a center instructor, as well as a reporter and photographer. In Spain, she founded Silver Press, a vehicle for distributing her photojournalism. In the world of flamenco, she became known as María la Marrurra, and one of her records gained considerable popularity among fans of the genre. Marrurra frequented the flamenco venues where Diego del Gastor, Antonio Mairena, and Fernanda and Bernarda de Utrera would perform. These spots were also popular among a core of Communist sympathisers associated with Francisco Moreno Galván, José Meneses and Manuel Gerena, all of whom had been openly confronted by the Franco regime.

9   Another noteworthy case is that of a draftsman by the name of Nazario, a teacher at the school in Morón de la Frontera, as well as one of Diego's apprentices (and who will always consider Diego as his spiritual master) who came to know the work of the underground comic book artist Robert Crumb through the base. He went on to develop a personal style based on Crumb's work and later gained some notoriety through his lawsuit against Lou Reed for plagiarism in the cover artwork of *Take No Prisoners* (1979). Nazario's professional career culminated with the publication of *Anarcoma*, a graphic novel based on a transsexual superhero. He was also one of the more outspoken members of the Rrollo, an underground movement that served as an obvious precedent for the Movida in Madrid.

the U.S. funded development of the region also took place against the cultural backdrop of the Cold War. [7] However, for whatever reason, flamenco apparently fitted within the plans for aesthetic modernity, which the Americans affixed to Spanish culture. From the highly influential United States Cultural Center – itself closely linked to U.S. intelligence operations – a hothouse flamenco was lavished with an entire range of financial and human support. [8] Others arrived from Tangiers, including an American guitarist known as Cristo – with the blessings of Paul Bowles and funding from the Smithsonian Institution – to conduct research in ethnomusicology. They also came into contact with Diego del Gastor in Morón, many spending the rest of their lives in the orbit of this extraordinary personality.

It is obvious that the American base in Morón became something of a focal point for everything that happened in the town. Regardless of its source, the surplus of money – which fed the flamenco musicians and provided them with endless drink in their ongoing parties – all came from the American soldiers. Donn E. Pohren, the author of the highly flattering biography of Diego, *A Way of Life*, initially held an administrative position at the U.S. base in Torrejón de Ardoz. It was during this time, while living in Madrid, that he wrote his other works *The Art of Flamenco* (1962) and *Lives and Legends of Flamenco* (1964). He later transferred to Morón de la Frontera. The bases also inevitably became a centre for American counterculture, and soldiers as well as base radio stations played the jazz of Coltrane or the rock of Hendrix. This music eventually influenced an entire generation of young flamenco musicians, who went on to form such bands as Smash and Pata Negra and gain tremendous popularity on the national rock scene. Interestingly enough, these groups also drew from the guitar sounds of Diego del Gastor. [9]

Diego del Gastor also played a significant role in the local avant-garde arts scene. José María Moreno Galván, one of the most important art critics of the time – and also close to such art groups as El Paso and Dau al Set – was also the brother of Francisco Moreno Galván. Francisco would perform in Puebla de Cazalla, in the vicinity of Morón de la Frontera, which was a magnet for the new breed of flamenco protest singers, notably José Meneses (who would often be accompanied by Diego on guitar). Viola and Feito, two painters from the El Paso group who were flamenco fans, also became followers of Diego. However, perhaps Diego's most radical appearance at the time occurred during the *Encuentros de Pamplona*[10] festival in 1972, which closed with Diego el del Gastor y su grupo de gitanos de Morón de la Frontera. The critics were enthralled with this performance, and there is a famous photograph of John Cage watching Los Morón de la Frontera. Despite the outstanding reception given Diego, the musician remained most taken by a single memory: "They brought me to the University of Pamplona where there was a huge crowd, all young people, all the hippest people, who had come to hear me. These were university students, people with an education". The festival met with opposition from what was then a clandestine Communist party, as well as the Basque separatist ETA, which reputedly planted a bomb. The Pamplona concerts tended to attract a radical and experimental element, one that was not clearly aligned with any particular political movement. Anthropologist José Antonio González Alcantud[11] – who was quite close to anthropological scholar Mimi Kaprow, Allan Kaprow's sister – viewed this phenomenon from an ethnographic standpoint, as arising from the attraction among modern young people to music which they might consider folkloric, communal or collective, particularly from Andalusia. At a certain point, an experimental mode of radical nihilism began to take hold, one that was directed toward the East – Buddhism, Zen, Tao, etc. – and which had John Cage as its foremost proponent. This movement eschewed European nihilism, one centred on Communist ideology, as most radically exemplified by German Dadaism. According to Alcantud, this new form of nihilism represented by Cage, Kaprow or Alan Watts domesticated the linguistic distortions of Dadaism, rendering them more productive, and thereby hegemonic in nature. When guitarist Cristo arrived in Morón de la Frontera, he wrote to Bowles about the overall permissiveness, drug use and communal life among the gypsies: "nothing, not a trace," – the American writer would later report from Tangiers – "of the Civil War or Lorca as I had expected".

By first confronting the paradoxical landscape which Darcy Lange experienced in his relationship with Diego del Gastor in Morón de la Frontera we may gain a better understanding of how flamenco came to function in his work, and why it became such a radically determining factor. We should begin by emphasising that Lange was a tremendous interpreter of the guitar styles he learned though Diego del Gastor. Even the gestures and flourishes he displayed when picking up a guitar bear the imprint of Diego.

Darcy Lange and Alyson Hunter in Morón de la Frontera, Spain, ca.1970.

10 The Encuentros de Pamplona, which was sponsored by the Huarte family, patrons of the arts who also fostered the independence of Jorge Oteiza and Pablo Palazuelo, was the main experimental arts event in Spain. Works were exhibited by Nauman, Ruscha, Muntadas, Weiner, Acconci, Oppenheim, Zaj, Valcárcel Medina, Oiticica, On Kawara, Morris, Downey, Dibbets, De Maria, Kosuth, Burgin and Art and Language, and Steve Reich, Luis de Pablo, Eduardo Polonio, Sylvano Bussotti, Mauricio Kagel, John Cage and David Tudor, among many others, also performed there.

11 José Antonio González, *Alcantud El Rapto del Arte, Antropología Cultural del Deseo Estético*, Universidad de Granada, 2002.

Flyer for flamenco guitar performance at the ICA London, 13 May, 1976.

12 Georges Didi-Huberman, *Ante el Tiempo*, Editorial Adriana Hidalgo, Buenos Aires, 2006; Carl Einstein, *La Escultura Negra y Otros Escritos*, Editorial Gustavo Gili, Barcelona, 2002.

13 *People of the World* (1983) also reveals this sort of holistic stance on various levels. The project brought together musical talent from a range of countries – the Netherlands, Spain, Greece, Turkey, Suriname and Indonesia – all with their own traditional folkloric roots, some even bearing similarities to flamenco. From an ideological standpoint the project also had a clear objective, that of using the traditional music of these immigrant groups in the Netherlands to counteract the alienation and marginalisation suffered by these groups while at the same time fostering a positive experience of sharing diverse cultural traditions.

In short, he was a good flamenco guitarist. It is true that Diego's technical level was quite distant from other schools – those of Montoya, Niño Ricardo or Sabicas – which eventually fed into the stylistic revolution led by Paco de Lucía, and which continue to have an impact on guitarists to this day. In this regard, Lange's musical style might be seen as anachronistic, however perhaps it is here, in this anachronism – in the sense defined by Carl Einstein [12] – that there arises in art a need to superimpose two different temporalities, confronting one with the other, in order to open a different temporal window in the present, and it was here that we find a key to Lange's interest in the gypsies and in flamenco.

It is also interesting to draw certain parallels between the unique toque or guitar sound of Morón and Lange's camerawork. A close consideration of this sound might help us to establish certain structural affinities between guitar style and the camera rhythms in such videos as *A Documentation of Bradford Working Life, UK*; *Cantavieja, Study of Work in a Spanish Village, Spain*; or *Waitara Freezing Works, Taranaki*. Here we find an elemental technique: a concept of slow rhythm, measured pauses, spare ornamentation, economy of means; non-harmonising melodies marked only by single-finger plucking (the style attributed to Diego and known as 'cuerda pelá'), tempos marked by bass flourishes, legatos, sustenutos and vibratos; an exacting sense of tempo, establishment of a canon, a measure and their repetition; themes that are drawn out; sustained adagios, the savouring of the precision and simplicity in each note; tempos framed by beat and rhythm; adjusting these guitar styles to the cante, or singing, with the guitar always at the service of the flamenco cantaor, yet strictly marking tempos, guiding the accompaniment rigorously along with the language, the lyrics. Diego's guitar sessions were long and canonically marked. It might seem as if he were continually retreading the same space, until he would hit upon a certain note, a bass chord, or a melody. Although strict, his system was also open and encompassing. As we have already noted, Diego's music could serve as an ideal vehicle for pairing flamenco with rock, jazz, son, reggae, or bossa nova. [13] Tempos were rigorously measured so that the very effort, the work involved, could be transmitted. These would also be framed by facial and bodily expressions that would settle dynamically into an overall sense of rapture or bliss. The relationship between musician and guitar is not instrumental, but almost prosthetic; in the act of performing or playing, the guitar

Antipodes: Darcy Lange, Work and Flamenco in the Image Chain of Production

would become an affixed appendage, a part of the musician's body, and in this sense there is a naturalising or humanising effect on what might otherwise be considered a tool. Everything becomes marked by tempo, by long yet highly measured planes. And so the point of contention between Diego and other flamenco singers would generally revolve around whether they could adhere to the tempo which he considered to be exact. And his problems with other guitarists were based on their tendency to bend the guitar to the whims of the singer, to the spectacle of the singer, or that they gave in to virtuosic flights of speed and overly complex falsetas, thus making the instrument into the object of spectacle itself. [14] As Mercedes Vicente has suggested, a parallel can be drawn between Diego's guitar techniques and Lange's instrumental approach to video, whereby the artist transforms video into a tool to be used by the very subjects he portrays. In this sense, Lange's work cannot be classified as documentary according to any standard definition, nor can it be labeled as a purely structuralist or conceptual exercise.

If, like Dan Graham, we listen closely enough to the soundtracks of Lange's videos, we can of course hear music. The punching of a calculator in *A Documentation of Bradford Working Life* which forms an almost piano counterpoint with the deafening background sounds of a factory, or the systematic harvesting of wheat in *Cantavieja*, with the melodic whistle of the scythe as it swings back and forth over the pasture. However there are forms of music other than those, which can be heard. There is a musical sense in the montage of images which often marks the tempos and rhythms of the work being documented. Rather than industrial music, we might consider this as work music – more akin to the early tonás or traditional melodies sung by toiling farm labourers, which are among the musical sources for flamenco, or the African-American spirituals of the Deep South – even if the backdrop nowadays might be that of a steel plant or a meat-processing factory. Strangely enough, metalwork and butchery are two mythic elements in the gypsy flamenco repertoire.

Although Lange's synopsis refers repeatedly to the resistance made by flamenco artists to the commercial banalisation of the time: consumerism, mass production, tourism, this message would have had far greater impact with the completion of *A Study of the Art of Flamenco as Work*. [15] Flamenco's own ambiguity inevitably failed to provide it with the adequate means to resist these factors. The way in which lives became organised

Fernanda Utrera and Diego del Gastor in Morón de la Frontera, Spain. Photograph by Bill Davidson.

Group of flamencos with Diego del Gastor (left, with guitar), Paso Ayala, Fernanda de Utrera, Andorrano, Joselero and others, late 1960s. Photograph by Bill Davidson.

14   Fernando González-Caballos Martínez Guitarras de cal, *Un Estudio Etnográfico del Toque de Morón*, Diputación de Sevilla, 2002.

15   Unpublished synopsis as it appears in a grant proposal. Courtesy of the Darcy Lange Archive, Govett-Brewster Art Gallery.

in the 1960s and 1970s, meant that these forms of economic commercialisation did negatively channel off interest without yet debilitating the flamenco way of life, its autonomy or communality. The framework of Lange's video cycles on forms of industrial and agricultural labour, as well as the way in which he presented work within a school or university context, would have positioned *A Study of the Art of Flamenco as Work* as a perfect consideration not only of flamenco but of art as work – if, indeed artistic activity can be considered as work per se – which he was presenting paradigmatically in the form of flamenco. The body of work that has been left by Lange is particularly illuminating, as few others are, of the evolution from industrial labour to cognitive labour – from *A Documentation of Bradford Working Life* to *Study of Three Birmingham Schools, UK* – the passage from proletariat to 'cognitariat', from material to information.

Nevertheless, Lange's *Cantavieja*, for example, is not diametrically opposed to *A Documentation of Bradford Working Life*. We find the same gestures, the same working tempos, despite the classic distinctions between rural and urban work environments. The relationships between worker and instrument, the gestures repeated time and again, the concatenation of tempo and the inevitable fruits of production, the deliberate wearing away of materials. During the 1970s, both of these groups of images were already somewhat anachronistic in nature, at least in the sense attributed by Carl Einstein – who also spent time in the Maestrazgo region while he was enlisted in the Durruti Column during the Spanish Civil War – of temporal friction. These are images that were already resuscitating a past moment at the time they were filmed. The relationships between work, body language and daily routines also establish certain parallels between *Bradford* and *Cantavieja*. Both works contain some essence of Courbet – and we should bear in mind that he was one of the first painters to depict flamenco artists in his portrait of *Adela Guerrero* (1851), an obvious precursor to Manet's *Lola of Valencia* – a reference which, along with the clear resonances of Millet's painting, Lange acknowledged and was proud of. [16] The same thing does not occur, however, in *Study of Three Birmingham Schools, UK* and *Studies of Teaching in Four Oxfordshire Schools, UK*, where the images are far closer to our own present world: multiracial classes, evolving attitudes between students and teachers, a work space based on exchange. There is also Lange's methodology: video recordings that were

16   A close reading of the relationships between work, time and daily routine in the paintings of Millet would also highlight the importance which that artist accorded to sex and repression in the libidinal economics of rural labour, aside from the obvious parallels which Salvador Dalí suggests in his reworking of Millet's *Angelus*. The poetry of flamenco cante often expresses the erotic subtext present in humanity's relationship with the natural environment, similar to themes that predominate in Renaissance pastoral poetry. It should be noted, however, that in reality, labour relationships in Andalusia have their own roots in slavery, and Lange would certainly have been aware of this perspective.

immediately watched by the subjects themselves who subsequently present their own reactions and opinions. What is involved here is the experience of education as work, and the gestures and body language are quite different. Relationships between tools or instruments also stand in contrast with previous works, and the music – or noise – does not emanate from industrial machinery or from animals toiling before a plough, instead, we now hear children and adults speaking, giggling, whispering, asking and responding to questions.

How did Lange's vision of flamenco as work evolve? We might arrive at our own conjectures if we follow the formal structuring of his videos. The element of anachronism is certainly there, perhaps a bit like Lewis Hine's photographs of the gypsies of Sarajevo, which although similar to many of the artist's portraits of immigrants and workers, nevertheless stand apart. There is something that jumps forth from their faces, evoking other times and circumstances. It also clearly has something to do with the imprint of work. As Arlette Farge [17] has observed, the lumpenproletariat is always proud of this imprint – mutilations quite often – which exempts it from having to share work, military service or other obligations with society. [18] We find ourselves in a system very similar to what Michel de Certeau describes in *The Practice of Everyday Life*, [19] an active and creative mode of consumption that is never submissive to the form of the product, the ingenious ways in which the weak make use of the strong, and the sensibility to create networks of intersubjectivity which are parallel to those of the established powers. For Lange's flamenco musicians, we understand the terms 'power,' 'strong' and 'product' to be equivalent to divisions of labour within Western industrialised societies. Anthropological studies of flamenco have also attempted to legitimise it as a mode of production, a form of work that 'produces' flamenco cante and baile. Such studies generally have a nationalistic subtext [20] – often unjustified or naïve, although this is not the time to refute them – which attempts to integrate flamenco into society, thus rehabilitating it as a form of work, without any exclusivity or marginality. Thus, the labourers from the field or from small factories are accorded their own useful recreational time for partying and art in the form of flamenco. And it is here that the gypsies occupy their own social space which, due to the triumph of these forms of song and dance, becomes socially integrated. In *A Study of the Art of Flamenco as Work*, Lange did in

17 Arlette Farge, *Efusión y Tormento, El Relato de los Cuerpos, Historia del Pueblo en el Siglo XVIII*, Katz, Buenos Aires, 2007.

18 Those who are part of the flamenco culture inhabit that terrain where the grotesque simultaneously separates them from society and binds them to the community in which they live. They are the dwarfs and the mutilated, the monstrous who Buñuel so masterfully portrayed at the margins of cityscapes like some part of the unconscious. Lange must have come into contact with Mellizo, Diego's brother. Mellizo, aside from being a guitarist, was also an alcoholic, a grotesque personage who used his 'homeliness' and wretched nature to avoid work, even guitar accompaniments at fiestas. Pohren was taken aback by the relationship the flamenco community had with the town's fools and mentally handicapped – they constantly poked fun at them, ridiculed them in the basest of ways, using such gestures to establish some veiled mark of separation. Both groups were equally useless when it came to productive work, yet a distinction had to be made: "we are the partyers and you are the fools". What Pohren saw as an Andalusian idiosyncrasy is nothing more than the vestige of lumpenproletariat social friction.

19 Michel de Certeau, *La Invención de lo Cotidiano*, Artes de Hacer, Universidad Iberoamericana, Mexico City, 1996.

20 Cristina Cruces, *Flamenco y Trabajo: un Análisis Antropológico de las Relaciones Entre el Flamenco y las Experiencias Cotidianas del Pueblo Andaluz*, Cabra, Ayuntamiento de Cabra, 1998; Estela Catania, *Flamencos de Gañania: una Mirada al Flamenco en los Cortijos Históricos del Bajo Guadalquivir*, Ediciones Giralda, Seville, 2007.

Darcy Lange and Maria Snijders in Peñíscola, Spain, ca. 1981. Photograph by Phil Slight

fact find himself with this dilemma. Previously we referred to the series *Rito y Geografía del Cante Flamenco*, which was produced for Spanish television between 1971 and 1973. The series was presented as a documentary on popular and flamenco music and therefore did not have to pass through the strict censorship that prevailed under Franco. The programme was thus able to provide a faithful and direct portrait of the slums of Madrid, Barcelona and Andalusia during those years, and of the areas where the flamenco community lived within the confines of marginalisation, an urban underworld inhabited by those excluded from the workforce.

The episodes devoted to Diego del Gastor in this series also highlighted another aspect that might have been of tremendous interest to Lange, specifically the teaching method that Diego applied in his private classes, at the school Pohren had set up on the Espartero estate. We have already discussed Diego's rudimentary guitar technique, and here, very un-mysteriously, after having his students go through half a dozen falsetas, he simply integrated them into his way of life. This was certainly a Socratic approach, one which drew most directly from the libertarian schools and middle class educational programmes established by the Institución Libre de Enseñanza. [21] According to Bergamín, he did not entirely believe in teaching rural labourers to read and write, since he felt that this would only lead to their exploitation and subjugation as part of the modern agricultural production apparatus. Instead he taught his own workers through a series of poetic games involving memorisation and recitation of verse, as well as preservation of the local dialectic vernacular applied specifically to work.

Inevitably it was this figure of the teacher as a real person, an idealist configuration of the model or an example to imitate – in this case Diego del Gastor – which would determine the success of these pedagogical experiments. This, of course, depended on how well pupils would assimilate and reconstruct by following the innovative and mechanical system of their master. Diego's foreign students [22] – particularly David G. Vogenitz, whose time in Morón also coincided with Darcy Lange's (1968 to 1969) – lavished praise on his talents as a teacher. During the week they would spend under his instruction, they would be included in the festivities where the great cantaores they admired were also performing. They learned by living, and this would mean by playing at one of the series of guitar gigs, while the centre for instructional methodology

21 Similar experiences had occurred with Gastor and others in Morón de la Frontera, during Spain's Second Republic. One of Diego's literary influences, Fernando Villalón, an eccentric and highly talented poet of noble lineage, who also had a somewhat surreal attitude toward life, shared a similar educational approach. Villalón had been a friend of Lorca, the renowned bullfighter Ignacio Sánchez Mejías, as well as other luminaries from Spain's Generation of 1927. As a cattle rancher, he experimented with a method for breeding green-eyed bulls.

22 David George Vogenitz, *The Flamenco Guitar*, Society of Spanish Studies, Berkeley, 1969.

Antipodes: Darcy Lange, Work and Flamenco in the Image Chain of Production

was essentially the fiesta. In this way, no one was actually aware of what they were learning – there was always a steady flow of alcohol, and quite a lot of hashish was smoked in the process as well. Nevertheless, the knowledge they did absorb would appear days later, once the fog of hangovers had lifted. They would be much discussion about what actually happened. "But, Diego, when did I learn this falseta?" Diego would try to get the partying started again, he would tell them how this or the other thing had happened, and assure them that they had indeed 'learned' that at the same fiesta. This way of teaching was undoubtedly of great interest to Darcy Lange. For an artist who so painstakingly examines the various aspects of the educational process in *Studies of Teaching in Three Birmingham Schools, UK*, this approach must have been absolutely fascinating. It is in this fascination that we can find also the shortcomings of a certain positivism. And it was the displacement of history by myth which Lange undoubtedly wished to confront with a critical eye.

Aside from Diego, there were other protagonists in Lange's work in Morón de la Frontera. These included Anzonini and Andorrano, as well as Joselero de Morón, Diego's brother-in-law. Fernandillo, another member of Diego's circle, was a gypsy who, according to Pohren, devoted far greater effort to finding a thousand and one ways not to work than actually showing up at the construction site where he was employed. One of his more famous sidelines was the 'watch swindle,' which involved unloading cheap knock-offs on nouveau riche types, and convincing them they were the proud owners of the most expensive watch in town. Sometimes he would spend endless amounts of time, with the inevitable invitations for drinks and other perks, in order to pocket what he might have otherwise earned from a regular work week. During times of crisis, Fernandillo never worried too much, since the local priest would always uncover some bits of jewellery or other baubles hidden in the church from the time the Marxists were sacking the town during the Civil War, and would pawn them and distribute the money among the poorest households.

I am relating all of this because such stories always circulated in Diego del Gastor's world, and it was this sense of mythic time that predominated, where events were based on neither truth nor fabrication, but tended to function on a mythic level. In the videos Lange was working on during the 1980s, *Aire del Mar* and *People of the World* (both of which deal with flamenco)

Darcy Lange and Maria Snijders, flamenco performance in New Zealand. Photograph by John Miller.

there is a focus on mythic displacement. The change in format from documentary reportage to happening: installation or performance is also significant. In this way, it would also seem that historic time was being abandoned for mythic time. And here we are talking about myth in two senses, at least – as time in allegorical or fantastic narratives, which is used as a means for explaining actual events. But also in the sense attributed by Roland Barthes, [23] as depoliticised speech which masks reality, where one's love for movie or soccer stars, tattoos or boxing, serve inevitably as a means for escaping reality. In Lange's work there is a tendency to repoliticise myth, and this occurs on two levels. His use of flamenco as an ongoing narrative, which for him might be coherent and compact, winds up triggering complete alienation – in the Brechtian sense of the word – on the part of the viewer.

To a certain extent this shift in Lange's work and tempo is entirely logical. This was a time of neo-conservatism, of a return to painting, to the forces of nature, to a reassertion of identity, and, essentially, a return to myth. Lange aims at the very heart of this tendency, providing a very different response. As Susan Buck-Morss has noted:

> The factory was the work-world counterpart of the opera house, a kind of counter-phantasmagoria that was based on the principle of fragmentation rather than on the illusion of wholeness. Marx's *Capital*, written in the 1860s, and thus contemporary with Wagner's operas, describes the factory as a total environment: Every sense organ is damaged to the same degree by the artificial elevation in temperature, by the by the dust-laden atmosphere, by the deafening noise, not to mention the danger to life and limb among the thickly crowded machinery, which, with the regularity of the seasons, issues its list of the killed and wounded in the industrial battle. [24]

It is obvious that if Lange were going to confront opera – and *Aire del Mar* is presented as an ecological media opera – he would have to use an approach that was completely opposed to Wagnerianism, a term which might be applied to the most reactionary manifestations of art which have triumphed from the 1980s onward, from Anselm Kiefer to Matthew Barney. For many reasons flamenco exhibits an all-encompassing understanding of life and

23   Roland Barthes, *Mitologías*, Siglo XXI editores, Mexico City, 1980.

24   Susan Buck-Morss, *Walter Benjamin, Escritor Revolucionario*, Interzona, Buenos Aires, 2005.

art that is diametrically opposed to the grandiose conceptions of the Wagnerian artwork. There is neither sufficient time nor space to adequately compare these two opposing views, however it may suffice to recall the diatribe that Nietzsche once launched against Wagner, and his own considerations on what Spain, Andalusia, and flamenco meant for modern aesthetics. Nietzsche would later confess that he had no special devotion to Bizet, however his opera *Carmen* beautifully capped off Nietzsche's argument. He says as much in the second section of *The Case of Wagner*, which I cite here at length:

> This work, too, redeems; Wagner is not the only 'redeemer'. With it, one says farewell to the damp North, to all the mists of the Wagnerian ideal. Already the plot saves us from it. It still has Mérimée's logic in its passion, the brevity of line, the hard necessity; it has, above all, what belongs to the more temperate climes, the clarity of the air, the 'limpidezza' of the air. Here, the climate is quite different in every respect. Here, another sensuality speaks, another sensibility, another serenity. This music is serene, but it is not a French or German serenity. Its serenity is African; doom hovers menacingly above it; its happiness is brief, sudden, without pardon. I envy Bizet's courage for this sensibility, which has not yet found expression in refined European music – for this more Southern, this browner, more sun-burnt sensibility ... How good to us are the golden afternoons of its happiness! Our gaze wanders off into the distance: have we ever seen a more placid sea? And how this Moorish dance soothingly speaks to us! How, in its lascivious melancholy, even our insatiability reaches the point of satiety, for once! Finally love, love that is translated back into nature! There is no elevation of the damsel, the virgin, or her highness. There is nothing of sentimentality. Not in love; instead we find fatality, cynicism, cruelty and innocence, and in all that, precisely, 'nature'! Love in its means, is war, and at its very foundation the mortal hatred of the sexes! ... Such a concept of love (the only one that is worthy of the philosopher) is rare: it distinguishes one work of art from thousands, since, on average, artists proceed in the same manner as the rest of the world, or even worse – they misunderstand love. Wagner has also misunderstood it. They even believe to be selfless

in it since they strive for advantage over another being, often against their own advantage. However, in exchange they want to own that other being. ... Even God makes no exception here. [25]

It would not take much effort to superimpose this text on *Aire del Mar*. [26] And as for working myths until they become politicised, flamenco does provide a good instrument. As Bení de Cádiz sang, in a tanguillo he composed in Cañamaque in 1947: "me escribe un amigo mío / que reside en el Japón / que la atómica le ha puesto / la nariz como un tapón." (*A friend of mine, who lives in Japan, has written me how the atom bomb made a cork of his nose*).

Finally, it is curious how flamenco functions in the works of Darcy Lange, as if it were essentially drawn from another extreme, the antipodes, of his interest in work, the culture of work, the gestures of work. "The atmosphere and the landscapes of Spain have greatly influenced me in my work," Lange confesses in his notes to *A Study of the Art of Flamenco as Work*. And by this we understand the fields, the small villages, the bars where gypsies would encamp for their festivities. When we see the footage Lange made of Diego del Gastor playing the guitar time and again, we see a fixed plane that stands insistently, perhaps eccentrically, in contrast with the images in the rest of his work. Images of the factory: images of the classroom. What is missing are the images of the fiesta, here in the form of flamenco, of the way Diego del Gastor and his buddies lived in an unending continuum of guitar playing, cante, baile, and drunken reverie. (Diego even imparted his own secrets for surviving three whole days of bingeing without ever getting drunk). What we do have, then, in terms of flamenco, is not an image, but perhaps an image in production. In terms of his constant approach to treating work, the production of images, when we apply this to flamenco, we have nothing more than the happening itself – its performance presence – forms that are continually fleeting, and which never manage to be productive. Perhaps *A Study of the Art of Flamenco as Work* was not completed because it was impossible to approach it in the terms Lange was accustomed to. It was material about work entirely opposed to everything this New Zealand artist had created up to this point. But it was also his life. That much can be seen in how he imitated Diego's gestures when he played the guitar. How he would twist his neck and close his eyes. This was a work from the depths. We might also note that if we could run a wire through the earth by

25 Friedrich Nietzsche, *El Caso Wagner, Nietzsche Contra Wagner*, Siruela, Madrid, 2002.

26 *Aire del Mar* also has its own political agenda, which cannot be thoroughly discussed at this time. Its political subtext is clearly pro-ecology in standpoint – denouncing the nuclear tests which the French government conducted in Polynesia in the early 1960s and referring to the 1985 South Pacific Forum ended in Rarotonga with the signing of the Nuclear Free Zone – and also highlights a positive, fraternal relationship with the environment, while supporting the territorial claims of the Māori and other Polynesian indigenous groups. The unique mythic level that operates in flamenco should also be taken into account in any reading of *Aire del Mar*.

Antipodes: Darcy Lange, Work and Flamenco in the Image Chain of Production

first puncturing the globe at Morón de la Frontera, in Andalusia, we would see how the other end would come out exactly at the opposite extreme in Urenui, Taranaki – Darcy Lange's birthplace in New Zealand.

Translation from Spanish by David Auerbach

Dan Graham, *Performer/Audience/Mirror*, 1977

De Appel, Amsterdam, the Netherlands.
Photograph by Darcy Lange.

Darcy Lange:
Great Artist and Friend

Dan Graham

Darcy Lange was a very important artist from the politically motivated video artistic generation of the 1970s. When we first met he told me his favourite artist was the countryside, French artist Jean-François Millet. I think of Darcy as a late 20th century Gustave Courbet – a man of the New Zealand countryside who became an 'avant-garde', urban, political artist. Like the 'post-hippie' late 1960s video artists, whose work I learned of through the magazine *Radical Software*, he used video, not only as documentary, but also as part of a learning process. Through the use of video feedback, Darcy sought to effect change in the people who were its subjects.

Darcy's work was, actually, closer to anthropology than to sociology. His work can be compared to the Chilean video artist, Juan Downey, who made agit-prop, anthropological videos of indigenous South American Indians. Darcy turned, in his later work, to the dispossessed Māori people of his own country. Both artists didn't merely study the people they documented, but attempted to provide tools to both effect social change and to re-contextualise their native cultures. Such a position builds on the work of the French anthropologist Claude Lévi-Strauss, in his book *Tristes Tropiques*.

Darcy's other love was playing flamenco guitar with Spanish gypsies. Back in New Zealand, he was close to his Māori friends. He was a gypsy at heart; Darcy's life-style when he was living in Europe was equally nomadic. Travelling from video shoot and to gallery exhibitions with his car and video equipment, he was typical of other younger artists from former colonies trying to deal with the modern 'old Europe'.

Darcy's work in the 1970s represented a subversive return to representational, socially relevant art forms. This meant going against the prevailing modernistic, abstract art. In this, his work was part of a new English, Marxist-influenced, art writing. Especially important here were the studies by T. J. Clark relating 19th century French socialist artists, like Courbet, to the industrial class struggle.

Darcy's work as a whole involved a non-reductive social critique. This is very different from the reductive dogmas of academic sociology and art criticism. His strategy was to combine the documentary tradition – which he admired in the 1930s photos of Dorothea Lange – with the 1960s video artists' interest in communication and feedback loops and also French structuralist models. To me, his best work was the *Work Studies in Schools* tapes, done with teachers in two contrasted cities: working class Birmingham and middle class, bourgeois, Oxfordshire. These videos provided feedback for the teachers themselves to help them improve their teaching skills.

Darcy was ambivalent about his middle class, land-owning New Zealand family. His mother, an amateur painter, loved Reagan, Thatcher and the Queen. Darcy's identification with the Māori indigenous people and his Marxism were attempts to undo his middle class values.

His approach to video was to treat it as a form of handicraft. His interest in folk music forms, like flamenco, was also seen in his choice of a car. He owned an old, classic Citroën Deux Chevaux. He was interested in communication with the 'others' in society and with 'outsider' artists (like me) as well as making music with other people – especially the 'other' people in the modernised Europe, like the gypsies. Darcy cared passionately about social justice. He was prone, at times, to a personal melancholy, 'cured' by (art) work and by playing his guitar. That Europe and New Zealand changed so much in the 1980s and 1990s 'business' culture hurt him deeply.

As a fellow, idealistic, young artist interested in media forms and as a good friend, Darcy would travel to my European performances and videotape them. Now is the right moment to fully appreciate Darcy's work. He desired to participate in a playful and community-based art. Darcy and I believed that life art could effect a harmonious mixture of work and play. My art and Darcy's was/is based on work that is part of the spectator's learning process.

Chronology

Andrew Clark & Alejandra Rojas

1946

Darcy Bruce Espie Lange born 22 September in Urenui, Aotearoa New Zealand.

1964

Moves to Auckland to study music at the University of Auckland but, dissatisfied with the programme for being too academic, transfers instead to Elam School of Fine Arts, where he studies sculpture.

At Elam he studies under the sculptor Jim Allen, head of the Sculpture Department at the time, *Life* magazine documentary photographer Tom Hutchins and the painters Colin McCahon and Robert Ellis.

Ellis, also a flamenco guitarist, introduces Lange to flamenco guitar.

Meets photographer Alyson Hunter, his first partner.

1966

Barry Lett Gallery, Auckland, group exhibition.

1967

Receives his Dip. F.A. Hons. from the University of Auckland's Elam School of Fine Arts.

>Barry Lett Gallery, Auckland, group exhibition.

1968

Arrives in London in September to study at the Royal College of Art.

Meets Phil Slight, New Zealand ex-pat painter and flamencologist, and close friend of American flamencologist Don Pohren, who introduces Lange to flamenco guitarist Diego del Gastor from Morón de la Frontera in Andalusia, Spain.

Auckland University acquires *Formality III*. Before its inauguration, the Govett-Brewster Art Gallery acquires *Extended Formality I*.

>Barry Lett Gallery, Auckland, group show.

>*Recent New Zealand Sculpture,* Auckland City Art Gallery.

1969

Travels with his brother Roger Lange to Morón de la Frontera, a place he visits frequently to study flamenco guitar with Diego del Gastor. They meet up with New Zealand video artist Phil Dadson.

1970

Receives a Queen Elizabeth II Arts Council grant.

Govett-Brewster Art Gallery acquires *Formality II*.

>*Young Contemporaries*, London, group exhibition.

>*Recent Acquisitions*, Govett-Brewster Art Gallery. *Extended Formality I* and *Formality II* are exhibited along with works by Colin McCahon, Ralph Hotere, Milan Mrkusich, Greer Twiss, Gordon Walters and Jim Allen.

1971

Graduates Master in Fine Arts from the Royal College of Art, London.

Starts using Super-8 film with wild sound documenting people at work.

Teaches at Birmingham Polytechnic between 1971 and 1973.

>*Darcy Lange*, Ikon Gallery, Birmingham, 16 November to 4 December (brochure).

1972

Phil Slight introduces Lange to video.

Produces his first video, *Breaker Metalworks*, in a factory in Birmingham.

Teaches in art colleges at Wolverhampton, Birmingham and Leicester.

>*A Survey of the Avant-Garde in Britain*, Gallery House, London, 2 to 15 October (catalogue).

1973
Death of Diego del Gastor.

Jack Wendler Gallery, London.

Europalia, Palais Des Beaux-Arts, Brussels, group show.

Six New Zealand Artists, New Zealand House, London, 13 to 23 February. Organised by Antoinette Godkin and Felicity Samuel Gallery.

1974
Separates from Alyson Hunter.

Death of his father.

Returns to New Zealand in September for six months.

Barry Lett Gallery, Auckland.

Projekt '74. Aspekte Internationaler Kunst am Anfang der 70er Jahre, curated by Wulf Herzogenrath, Köln, 6 July to 8 September (catalogue).

International Arts Festival for Chilean Resistance, organised by Artists for Democracy, composed by David Medalla, Cecilia Vicuna, John Dugger, and Guy Brett.

Six New Zealand Artists, organised by Antoinette Godkin, Auckland City Art Gallery (catalogue).

1975
Between 1975 and 1977, he travels extensively throughout New Zealand, Canada, the United States, Mexico and Europe.

Meets John Baldessari in Los Angeles and Dan Graham in Philadelphia.

Willoughby Sharp interviews him for *Avalanche*.

Signs contract with Howard Wise for Electronic Art Intermix to distribute his videos. For unknown reasons this does not materialise, possibly due to technical difficulties.

Artists' Video Tapes, Palais Des Beaux-Arts, Brussels, 25 February to 16 March (catalogue).

Six New Zealand Artists as part of 6th Mildura Sculpture Exhibition, Mildura, Victoria, Australia, April (catalogue).

The Video Show, Serpentine Gallery, London, 1 to 26 May (catalogue).

The Kitchen, New York, screenings 10 to 11 June.

Video V, curated by Barbara London, Museum of Modern Art, New York, August to October.

9e Biennale de Paris, 19 September to 2 November (catalogue).

95 Reade Street, New York, solo show.

Institute of Contemporary Arts, London, solo show.

British Film Institute, London.

Oppenheim Studio, Köln, solo show.

Art Fair, Köln.

1976
Appears in *Studio International Journal of Modern Art*, May.

Performs flamenco music at the Institute of Contemporary Arts, London, 13 May.

9e Biennale de Paris à Nice, 30 January to 31 March (catalogue).

A Documentation of Bradford Working Life, The Kitchen, New York, 24 February to 6 March.

Darcy Lange and Andrew Turner, Industrial Museum, Bradford Art Galleries and Museums, Bradford, 16 May to 13 June).

Venice Biennale

DARCY LANGE

november 16 – december 4

SWALLOW ST. BIRMINGHAM B5 4AA

Telephone: 021-643-0708

Manager: Jeanette Koch

Open Tuesdays to Saturdays 11 - 6

CONCEPTS AND APPROACH

I am making an intense study of the truths which are in our environment, the things of importance in the visual world. The intent is to capture and create upon a moment of memorable beauty or depth. The idea seems to be a way of devising an art diary through the translation of what one experiences, into sculpture.

There is a vast need for artistic consciousness which is orientated towards the visual environment. There is a need for an uninhibited investigation and communication with the world around us.

I am involved in the development of a social conscience, and a development of a record and memory of the physical world. Art seems to have become isolated. It is perhaps true that a bad understanding of our fellows could lead to uncommunicative art.

Because of the need to understand, there is the need to communicate. We need to create a reaction, as a reaction from the audience is needed by the artist, for him to begin to be able to judge his successes.

It is a vicious circle. The public, despite fifty years of abstraction and the knowledge and education of its existence, prefers to accept and feel an affinity with pictorial and representational art.

It is therefore reasonable that I have involved myself with a kind of representational approach. The necessity of communication may be questioned, but it seems that if the artist is going to feel justification for his work, he will need to have an audience. One cannot live and work in a vacuum.

EXHIBITION OF PREVIOUS & PRESENT WORK BY DARCY LANGE

Born New Zealand 1946
Studied at the Royal College of Art

EXHIBITIONS: 1. Reconstruction of workers
2. Art films & photographs

INVITATION
The Directors cordially invite you to the
PREVIEW of this exhibition on
Monday, November 15 at 7·30 pm. - coffee

Bradford Art Galleries and Museums

DARCY LANGE & ANDREW TURNER

Photographs and Video   Paintings, Drawings and Prints

16 May - 13 June 1976
Industrial Museum
Moorside Road Eccleshill Bradford BD2 3HP
Open Daily 10·00-17·00

Flyer for solo exhibition at Ikon
Gallery, Birmingham, November 16 to
December 4, 1971.

*A Documentation of Bradford Working
Life*, The Kitchen, New York City, 1976.

Brochure for Bradford Art Galleries and
Museums, *A Documentation of Bradford
Working Life*, 1976.

Chronology

1977

Wins grant from Artists' Film and Video Committee at the Arts Council of Great Britain for *Film Studies in Comprehensive and Grammar Schools* (not finished).

Returns to New Zealand in June and leaves again in mid-December.

Starts *Māori Land Project* and records at Bastion Point and related material concerning the Ngatihine Block case.

Visits New Zealand painter Tom Kreisler in Mexico.

A Documentation of Bradford Working Life, Institute of Contemporary Arts, London.

Work Studies in Schools, curated by Mark Francis, Museum of Modern Art Oxford (catalogue). Invited by director David Elliot.

1978

In February returns to London after a few days stopover in New York.

Spends time in Amsterdam and works with René Coelho on *Māori Land Project*.

From July to September continues work on *Māori Land Project* in New Zealand.

In October teaches at the Nova Scotia College of Art and Design (NSCAD) in Halifax after an invitation by Dan Graham. Lange teaches along with artists Dara Birnbaum, Jeff Wall, Amy Taubin, Michael Asher and Martha Rosler.

Lectures at the Academy of Fine Arts, Design and Architecture (AKI), Enschede, the Netherlands in November.

Returns to New Zealand via Vancouver in late November.

Darcy Lange: New Video Works, Art Metropole, Toronto, screening 27 January.

Video Analysis – Māori Land Issue, Montevideo, Amsterdam, 27 March to 6 April.

Darcy Lange: The Long Take, curated by Ron Brownson, Auckland City Art Gallery.

1979

In New Zealand continues working on *Māori Land Project*.

Leaves for the Netherlands in mid-February to teach at AKI and work on *Bastion Point* with Leonard Henny, from the Centre for International Media Research in Utrecht.

During August and September lives in Peñíscola in Spain, with New Zealand artist Keith Paterson.

The Historical Archive of Contemporary Arts (ASAC) of the Venice Biennale purchases and distributes Lange's tapes from Art/Tapes 22 of Florence (videotapes previously owned by Mrs. Bicocchi).

Auckland City Art Gallery, group show.

Lives, Hayward Gallery, London, group show (catalogue).

1980

Flies to the Netherlands from Canada in September.

Along with Colin Clark, participates in the Fourth Russell Tribunal in Rotterdam and records it as part of *Māori Land Project*.

Meets Maria Snijders in Utrecht.

Between 1980 and 1983 performs flamenco guitar in the Netherlands.

Returns to New Zealand later in the year.

Het Land van de Māori, Van Abbemuseum, Eindhoven, 12 January to 10 February (catalogue). Invited by Jan Debbault and Rudi Fuchs.

Māori Land Project, Internationaal Cultureel Centrum, Antwerp, March to April (catalogue).

1981

AKI Enschede Musical Art Students, the Netherlands.

1982

Returns to New Zealand with Maria Snijders, where they marry in Urenui on 10 April.

Darcy Rafael Collin Lange is born on 24 September in Tilburg, the Netherlands.

LAND
WORK
PEOPLE

DARCY LANGE SURVEY

4 APRIL – 5 MAY 1985

GOVETT–BREWSTER
ART GALLERY
NEW PLYMOUTH

Poster for *Land Work People, Darcy Lange Survey*, Govett-Brewster Art Gallery, New Plymouth, 4 April to 5 May, 1985.

Darcy Lange and John Miller, New Zealand, mid-1980s.

Flyer for *Māori Land Project* at the Van AbbeMuseum, Eindhoven and Internationaal Cultureel Centrum, Antwerp, 1980.

DARCY LANGE

'Het land van de Maori'

12.01 t/m 10.02.80

Van Abbemuseum
Bilderdijklaan 10
5611 NH Eindhoven/ Nederland

U bent van harte welkom
op de opening op vrijdag
11 januari van 20.00 tot 21.30 uur

Chronology

Land Work People, Darcy Lange Survey,
at Govett-Brewster Art Gallery, 1985.
Photographs by John Miller.

1983
Accompanies Chari Lopez at festivals in Jaen, Spain.

Govett-Brewster Art Gallery (director Dick Bett) acquires Lange's whole video oeuvre from the 1970s onwards, plus related material such as correspondence, photographs and exhibition catalogues.

Performs *People of the World* at six concerts in the Netherlands.

> *Saki*, group exhibition, Enschede, the Netherlands, Dauerleihagbe Ingrid Oppenhein, Städtisches Kunstmuseum Bonn (catalogue).

1984
Returns to New Zealand with Maria and son Darcy.

Rawinia Anna Elyson Lange born on 9 November in New Plymouth.

Between 1984 and 1986 he performs at Taranaki schools, and in theatres, and private houses throughout New Zealand.

1985
Land Work People, Darcy Lange Survey, Govett-Brewster Art Gallery, 4 April to 5 May.

1986
Teaches at the Otara Community Centre, Auckland.

> *A New Peace*, Artwork, Auckland, 11 to 22 August.

1988
Aire del Mar performed at Govett-Brewster Art Gallery; Sarjeant Art Gallery, Wanganui; City Art Gallery, Wellington; The Bath House, Rotorua; Artspace, Auckland, and Maidment Theatre, University of Auckland.

1989
Between March and July he travels to Vancouver, New York, Frankfurt, Amsterdam and Los Angeles. In July he returns to New Zealand.

1990
Guest at the Peña Flamenca in Jaen, Spain.

> *Two Years of New Zealand Landscape Art*, Artspace, Auckland.

1992
Concert by Paco Campana and Maria Snijders, Pumphouse, North Shore.

> *Aire del Mar* performed by Paco Campana, Maria Snijders and Chilean poet Esteban Espinoza, Auckland Town Hall Concert Chamber.

> *Art and Organised Labour*, City Art Gallery, Wellington.

1993
Separates from Maria and children.

> *Aire del Mar* performed by Paco Campana, Maria Snijders and Denys Trussel, The Maidment Theatre, University of Auckland, 8 and 9 July.

1994
Aire del Mar performed at the Gus Fisher Gallery, Auckland.

1995
Work Studies, Auckland Art Gallery.

1998
Begins *Artists, Musicians and Poets at Work* (completed in 2000).

> *Action Replay: Post-Object New Zealand Art*, Artspace, Auckland; Govett-Brewster Art Gallery and Auckland Art Gallery.

1999
Homenaje a Garcia Lorca, concert by Paco Campana, Marco Basilisco de Estepona, Denys Trussel, Esteban Espinoza and Veronica de Maya. Auckland Town Hall Concert Chamber, 10 July.

> *The Māori Land Project*, Auckland War Memorial Museum.

> *PALeo Neo Video: Chapters from the History of Video Art in New Zealand 1970s – 1990s*, curated by Lawrence McDonald, Film Centre, Wellington.

2000

Māori Land Project acquired by the Auckland War Memorial Museum.

Interview with Jacqueline Bullmore acquired by Te Papa as part of the Ted Bullmore archive.

Māori Land Project, Auckland War Memorial Museum.

2001

Sangre Flamenca, performance by Paco Campana, Charo de Luna, Rosa Toledo, Antonio Soria, Denys Trussel and Esteban Espinoza. Auckland Town Hall Concert Chamber, 23 June.

2002

Flamenco Gitano, Flamenca Rumba Arabesque, performance by Paco Campana, Charo de Granada, Gazpacho, Kojo Owuso, Trishna de Bali, Denys Trussel, Esteban Espinoza and Yuyai Lima de Peru. Auckland Town Hall Concert Chamber, 22 June.

2003

Viaje de las Palomas, performance by Paco Campana, Charo de Luna, Veronica de Maya, Marco Basilisco, Denys Trussel, Esteban Espinoza. Special Guests: Andorrano de Moron, Pepe del Gastor, Manolo Canalejas, Manolo Varela. Auckland Town Hall Concert Chamber, 7 February.

A Century of Artists' Film in Britain, curated by David Curtis, Tate Britain, London.

2004

Lights>Camera>Action: Critical Moments from the Govett-Brewster Collections 1969–2004, Govett-Brewster Art Gallery.

2005

Darcy Lange dies of pneumonia on 8 August in Auckland.

2006

Viewfinder: Four Decades of the Govett-Brewster Art Collection, Govett-Brewster Art Gallery, 18 March to 7 May.

Darcy Lange: Study of an Artist at Work, curated by Mercedes Vicente, Govett-Brewster Art Gallery, 29 July to 24 September.

2007

'Work Studies in Schools', *Documenta12 Magazine* No. 3, as part of *Natural Selection* magazine edited by David Hatcher (catalogue).

Darcy Lange: Study of an Artist at Work travels within Taranaki to Fritz Reuter Gallery, Inglewood, 20 December to 14 January and Percy Thompson Gallery, Stratford, 11 February to 14 March and to Adam Gallery, Wellington, 23 March to 13 May.

Films in Real Time 1970–9, screening programme organised by Mark Williams. Films by Phil Dadson, Bruce Barber, Darcy Lange and others. Anthology Film Archives, New York, October; Nova Scotia College of Art and Design, Halifax, October; and Chicago Film-makers Co-operative, November.

2008

Films in Real Time 1970–9, screening, New Zealand Film Archive Media Theatre, Wellington, 13 March.

You and Me, Sometimes, curated by Sandra Antelo-Suarez, Lehman Maupin Gallery, New York (screening introduced by Dan Graham and Lori Zippay).

The Great Game to Come, screening, curated by Chus Martinez, Frankfurter Kunstverein, Frankfurt, 13 to 21 May.

Work Studies in Schools, co-curated by Mercedes Vicente and Helen Legg, Ikon Gallery, Birmingham, in partnership with Govett-Brewster Art Gallery.

Darcy Lange: Study of an Artist at Work, at Govett-Brewster Art Gallery, July 29 to September 24, 2006. Photographs by Bryan James.

List of Works

Alejandra Rojas

Lange considered his work as an ongoing documentation rather than 'final work'. Even though in some works, such as *A Documentation of Bradford Working Life, UK* and *A Documentation of Calverton and Pleasley Coalmining Communities, Nottingham, UK*, he clearly stated the use of photography, film, and video as intrinsic to the work, in most instances there is a degree of indeterminacy about the status and role of different media and contents. With this in mind the descriptions given below are inclusive, indicating the existence of such materials without prescribing a conclusive definition of what constitutes each work.

1966

Unnamed Monster
Steel and lacquer, dimensions unknown.
Large-scale abstract geometric sculpture. This work no longer exists.

Scarlet Chrome
Steel and lacquer, dimensions unknown.
Large-scale abstract geometric sculpture. This work no longer exists.

1967

Extended Formality I
Steel and lacquer, 2.3m x 4m x 6m.
Govett-Brewster Art Gallery.
Large-scale abstract geometric sculpture.

> *Recent New Zealand Sculpture*, Auckland City Art Gallery, 1968.
> *Recent Acquisitions*, Govett-Brewster Art Gallery, 1970.
> *Land Work People, Darcy Lange Survey*,
> Govett-Brewster Art Gallery, 1985.
> *Darcy Lange: Study of an Artist at Work*,
> Govett-Brewster Art Gallery, 2006.

Formality I
Steel and lacquer, 1m x 1m x 2m.
Govett-Brewster Art Gallery.
Large-scale abstract geometric sculpture.

> *Recent Acquisitions*, Govett-Brewster Art Gallery, 1970.
> *Land Work People, Darcy Lange Survey*,
> Govett-Brewster Art Gallery, 1985.
> *Darcy Lange: Study of an Artist at Work*,
> Govett-Brewster Art Gallery, 2006.

Formality II
Steel and lacquer, 6.1m x 5.6m x 4.9m.
Museum of New Zealand Te Papa Tongarewa.
Large-scale abstract geometric sculpture.

> *Recent New Zealand Sculpture*, Auckland City Art Gallery, 1968.
> *Land Work People, Darcy Lange Survey*,
> Govett-Brewster Art Gallery, 1985.

Formality III
Steel and lacquer, 2.1m x 2.2m x 6.2m.
The John Weeks Trust AUSA.
Large-scale abstract geometric sculpture.

> *Recent Acquisitions*, Govett-Brewster Art Gallery, 1970.
> *Land Work People, Darcy Lange Survey*,
> Govett-Brewster Art Gallery, 1985.
> *Darcy Lange: Study of an Artist at Work*,
> Govett-Brewster Art Gallery, 2006.

1969

Untitled (Composition and Realism with Coat)
Steel, lacquer and fibreglass, dimensions unknown.
Large-scale sculpture combining abstract geometric with figurative realistic elements. Produced at the Royal College of Art, this work no longer exists.

> *Land Work People, Darcy Lange Survey*,
> Govett-Brewster Art Gallery, 1985
> (showed photographs documenting the work).
> *Darcy Lange: Study of an Artist at Work*,
> Govett-Brewster Art Gallery, 2006
> (photo documentation).

Untitled
(Composition and Realism with Chair and Still Life)
Fabric, fibreglass and chromium-plated bronze, dimensions unknown.
Large-scale sculpture combining abstract geometric and figurative elements. Produced at the Royal College of Art, this work no longer exists.

> *Land Work People, Darcy Lange Survey*,
> Govett-Brewster Art Gallery, 1985
> (showed photographs documenting the work).
> *Darcy Lange: Study of an Artist at Work*,
> Govett-Brewster Art Gallery, 2006
> (photo documentation).

Untitled (Chromed Still Life and Modelling Stand)
Chromium-plated bronze and steel,
dimensions unknown.
Large-scale sculpture combining abstract geometric and
figurative elements. Produced at the Royal College of Art,
this work no longer exists.

> *Land Work People, Darcy Lange Survey*,
> Govett-Brewster Art Gallery, 1985
> (photo documentation).

1970
Environment of Mokau and Reminiscence
Wood, acrylic and chromium-plated bronze,
dimensions unknown.
Large-scale environmental work combining abstract
geometric and figurative elements, and life-size human
figures set against a painted backdrop with references to
Mokau's sea landscape on the west coast of New Zealand.
Produced at the Royal College of Art, this work no
longer exists.

> *Land Work People, Darcy Lange Survey*,
> Govett-Brewster Art Gallery, 1985
> (showed photographs documenting the work).
> *Darcy Lange: Study of an Artist at Work*,
> Govett-Brewster Art Gallery, 2006
> (photo documentation).

1971
Stonehenge and Bourgeoisie
Fibreglass, acrylic paint, and chromium-plated bronze,
dimensions unknown.
Large-scale environmental work combining abstract
geometric elements and figurative elements. Produced at
the Royal College of Art, this work no longer exists.

> *Land Work People, Darcy Lange Survey*,
> Govett-Brewster Art Gallery, 1985
> (photo documentation).

Commentary – Equality
Fibreglass, wood, scaffolding steel, dimensions unknown.
Large-scale work. Produced at the Royal College of Art,
this work no longer exists.

> *Land Work People, Darcy Lange Survey*,
> Govett-Brewster Art Gallery, 1985
> (photo documentation).

Irish Roadworkers
Fibreglass, wood, scaffolding steel, slides, sound.
Sculptural installation with life-size, realistic
representations of the Irish road workers repairing
London's Oxford Street. Surrounding these figures
are four screens with projected colour slides showing
the traffic on the street; two of the projectors operated
with dissolve units to mimic movement. The work was
accompanied by a wild sound recording. This was Lange's

thesis for the Royal College of Art and his last sculptural
work. It was exhibited at Ikon Gallery, Birmingham in
1971, in his first solo exhibition in the UK. This work no
longer exists.

> *Darcy Lange*, Ikon Gallery, Birmingham, 1971.

Social Consideration, Communication and Observation
Six super-8 films, colour and b/w photographs, with wild
sound. Darcy Lange Estate.
3 mins to 8 mins films accompanied by a sound track
from a tape recorder. Each film is done in a single shot.
They are all studies of people at work: a woman putting
out her washing in London; a hardware store employee
in South Kensington; farmers burning wheat in Kent;
a man milking cows in Sussex; a cattle auction in a
market outside Bradford; and the transport café, 'Pini's
Restaurant', in London.

1972
Studies of Family Groups, UK
Two 16mm films, b/w photographs, synchronised sound,
30 mins each. Darcy Lange Estate.
Two studies of families from different class backgrounds
and their eating habits. One film shows a middle class
family and the other a working class family. Originally
the work was designed to include a third study of an
agricultural family. The films are almost still lifes, the
camera only moves twice, once to zoom in after the first
eight minute long shot and then again to zoom back out
eight minutes before the end. Lange's intention was to
capture and compare, through a natural and objective
observation, interesting differences in personalities and
mannerisms according to class. Basil Cox filmed in Maida
Vale, London in February. Mr. and Mrs. Mates and Family
Filmed in Kent House, Pimlico, London in April.

> *A Survey of the Avant-Garde in Britain*, Gallery House, London, 1972.

*Five Working Studies in British Factories
and Workplaces, UK*
Video, colour and b/w photographs, sound, 114 mins.
Darcy Lange Estate and Govett-Brewster Art Gallery.
These videos depict working life in five factories in
England. They record both working and leisure time
in an attempt to show the atmosphere in the factory
and the personalities of the people involved. They also
show people joking directly to the camera, and in some
instances interviews with the subjects portrayed.

Breakers Metalworks, Balsall Heath, Birmingham
This is Lange's first video. In addition to shots of workers,
there is a short interview with the factory owner.

E. Brennan General Woodcarving Furniture
Workshop, London
This factory was opposite Lange's studio.

Wild, Mellor and Bromley, Leicester
He recorded this video with Sony's first ½ inch video
recorder. Portrays work at a knitting factory.
Marbett Manufacturing Co. Ltd., London
Images of people working at a furniture store.

Burns and Lux, London
Clothing factory.

> *A Survey of the Avant-Garde in Britain*, Gallery House, London, 1972.
> *Land Work People, Darcy Lange Survey,*
> Govett-Brewster Art Gallery, 1985

Allotment Gardens
Video, b/w photographs, sound, 52 mins.
Darcy Lange Estate and Govett-Brewster Art Gallery.
These studies were made near Dagenham highway on
the way through the East End of London, and in Barnsley,
South Yorkshire.

> *Land Work People, Darcy Lange Survey,*
> Govett-Brewster Art Gallery, 1985.
> *Darcy Lange: Study of an Artist at Work,*
> Govett-Brewster Art Gallery, 2006.

1973
A Documentation of Calverton and Pleasley Coalmining
Communities, Nottingham, UK
Double 16mm film looped, video 45 mins, photographs,
and transcript of recorded interview 120 mins. Darcy
Lange Estate and Govett-Brewster Art Gallery.
This project documents the lives of Calverton and Pleasley
coalminers in Nottingham soon after the success of the
1973 strike. It originally comprised films, photographs,
videotapes, a sound recording, and a transcript. The
sound recording is lost, but the transcript provides part
of the information recorded on it. Although Lange had
abandoned sculpture in favour of film and video, his early
interest in the discipline is still evident in the way he chose
to exhibit this work at the Govett-Brewster Art Gallery in
1985. The two four minute films were displayed in 40-metre
loops that created a three-dimensional structure and were
then simultaneously projected onto a split screen.

> *Six New Zealand Artists*, New Zealand House, London, 1973;
> Auckland City Art Gallery, 1974 (the film included in this
> exhibition was 30 minutes long and was not looped).
> *Land Work People, Darcy Lange Survey,*
> Govett-Brewster Art Gallery, 1985.
> *Darcy Lange: Study of an Artist at Work,*
> Govett-Brewster Art Gallery, 2006.

Craigdarrock, Scotland
Video, b/w photographs, sound, 90 mins. Darcy Lange
Estate and Govett-Brewster Art Gallery.
These are studies of a day's work for shepherds on a sheep
run called Craigdarrock in a village in Dumfrieshire,
Scotland. The first study documents Alec, one of the
shepherds, as he gathers his sheep. The second study begins
with a view from afar of the sheep gathering (the camera
filming from a hill across the valley) but eventually the sheep
pass close to the camera as they go on their way towards the
yards. The third study records the work in the yards. Here, the
shepherds sort the sheep, put identity marks on their ears,
clip their feet, crutch them, and castrate some of the males.
Later the shepherds have their lunch and free the sheep.

> Jack Wendler Gallery, London, 1973.
> *Projekt '74, Aspekte Internationaler Kunst am Anfang*
> *der 70er Jahre*, Köln, 1974 (2 cassettes totalling 90 mins).
> *Dauerleihagbe Ingrid Oppenhein,*
> Städtisches Kunstmuseum Bonn, 1983 (80 mins).
> *Land Work People, Darcy Lange Survey,*
> Govett-Brewster Art Gallery, 1985.
> *Darcy Lange: Study of an Artist at Work,*
> Govett-Brewster Art Gallery, 2006.

1974
A Documentation of Bradford Working Life, UK
Colour and b/w photographs, sound, 16mm film, video,
145 mins. Darcy Lange Estate and Govett-Brewster
Art Gallery.
This work comprises studies of people working in four
factories in Bradford: a steel melting factory, a wool mining
company, a piston and piston ring factory, and a mail
order warehouse. Interested in exploring the aesthetic and
formal differences between film, video, and photography,
Lange documented his subjects using the three media.
Indeed, film and video were recorded simultaneously
and with the same framing. Each study is videotaped for
10 minutes, and filmed for the first 30 seconds and the
last 30 seconds of the videotaped scene. Lange wanted
to show this work in the factories where it was recorded,
but was not granted permission because of the perceived
controversial nature of the material. Even though Bradford
Art Galleries and Museums commissioned the work, its
exhibition at the Bradford Industrial Museum was delayed
until 1976 for the same reason.

The First Situation
Osborne Steels Ltd., Low Moore, a steel melting works.
1st Study: 'Rolling Mill' – N. Magloire, O. Moyston,
K. Harper, J. Charington, C. Teleamuque, R. Martin,
F. Pashley, D. Robertshaw, B. Cook, A. Josephe.
2nd Study: 'The Grinding' – Leon Frazier, Godfrey Broadbent.
3rd Study: 'Furnaces' – Charley Helps, Alan Wright,
Harry Barraclough.

The Second Situation
Whiteheads Woollen Mills.
1st Study: 'French Combing' – Mrs. O' Connor.
2nd Study: 'Traditional Combing' – Alah Dad.
3rd Study: 'Spinning' –Mrs. Alice Jennings.
4th Study: 'Spinning' – Theresa Hird.

The Third Situation
Hepworth and Grandage Ltd, England's largest producers of pistons and piston rings.
1st Study: 'The Verson Press' – Roy Penny.
2nd Study: 'Piston Inspection' – Miss June Bell.
3rd Study: 'Dual Lathes' – Albert Ozolins.

The Fourth Situation
Grattan Ltd, a large mail order warehouse.
1st Study: 'Study of a Packer' – John Wood.
2nd Study: 'Study of a Packer' – Burford Maunders.
3rd Study: 'Order Assembly' – Michael Normington.
4th Study: 'Order Assembly' – Kevin Bulmer.
5th Study: 'Punch Card Operator' – Janet Thornton.

> *The Video Show*, Serpentine Gallery, London, 1 to 26 May 1975 (showed 12 mins of study of Roy Penny).
> Art Fair, Köln, 1975
> (appears in the catalogue as 3 60 min cassettes).
> *Video V*, Museum of Modern Art, New York, 1975 (showed 12 mins of study of Roy Penny).
> *A Documentation of Bradford Working Life*, The Kitchen, New York, 1976.
> *9e Biennale de Paris*, 19 September to 2 November 1975.
> *Darcy Lange & Andrew Turner*, Industrial Museum, Bradford Art Galleries and Museums, Bradford, 16 May to 13 June 1976.
> *9e Biennale de Paris à Nice*, 1976.
> *Darcy Lange: A Documentation of Bradford Working Life*, Institute of Contemporary Arts, London, 1977.
> *Dauerleihagbe Ingrid Oppenhein*, Städtisches Kunstmuseum Bonn, 1983. In the catalogue the work appears as *A Documentation of Bradford Working Life I* (58 mins), *A Documentation of Bradford Working Life II* (55 mins), and *A Documentation of Bradford Working Life III* (40 mins).
> *Land Work People, Darcy Lange Survey*, Govett-Brewster Art Gallery, 1985.
> *Darcy Lange: Study of an Artist at Work*, Govett-Brewster Art Gallery, 2006.

Jack Jury, Stockman, Uruti, Taranaki
Video, b/w photographs, sound, 41 mins.
Darcy Lange Estate and Govett-Brewster Art Gallery.
Studies of Jack Jury, a stockman whom Lange had known since childhood, and who worked on Lange's father's farm in Taranaki, New Zealand. There are shots of work and leisure time.

> *Darcy Lange: Study of an Artist at Work*, Govett-Brewster Art Gallery, 2006.

Hewa, Study of a Māori Tree-feller at Waitaanga, King Country
Video, b/w photographs, sound, 28 mins.
Darcy Lange Estate and Govett-Brewster Art Gallery.
Studies of a tree felling in Waitaanga, King Country, New Zealand. Lange records both work and leisure time.

Work: study of a tree felling at Waitaanga, King Country.
Personalisation: recording of lunch with the tree-feller.

> *The Long Take*, curated by Ron Brownson, Auckland City Art Gallery, 1978.
> *Dauerleihagbe Ingrid Oppenhein*, Städtisches Kunstmuseum Bonn, 1983 (45 mins).
> *Land Work People, Darcy Lange Survey*, Govett-Brewster Art Gallery, 1985.
> *Darcy Lange: Study of an Artist at Work*, Govett-Brewster Art Gallery, 2006.

Clem Coxhead, Study of Cow Milking in Opunake, Taranaki
Video, b/w photographs, sound, 31 mins.
Darcy Lange Estate and Govett-Brewster Art Gallery.
Study of Clem Coxhead, a New Zealand dairy farmer. It records the gathering of the cows, the milking, the milked cows returning to thc paddock, and leisure time with Clem and his friends and family. Mount Taranaki (previously known as Mt. Egmont) can be seen in the background.

Work: study of cow milking in Opunake, Taranaki; recording with Mt. Egmont in the background.
Personalisation: evening with Clem; family and friends.

> *Artist's Video Tapes Palais des Beaux-Arts*, Brussels, 1975.
> Art Fair, Köln, 1975 (45 mins).
> *The Long Take*, curated by Ron Brownson, Auckland City Art Gallery, 1978.
> *Dauerleihagbe Ingrid Oppenhein*, Städtisches Kunstmuseum Bonn, 1983 (45 mins).
> *Land Work People, Darcy Lange Survey*, Govett-Brewster Art Gallery, 1985.
> *Darcy Lange: Study of an Artist at Work*, Govett-Brewster Art Gallery, 2006.

Waitara Freezing Works, Taranaki

Video, b/w photographs, sound, 90 mins.
Darcy Lange Estate and Govett-Brewster Art Gallery.
Studies of people at work in a slaughterhouse in New Zealand. This work shows the elegance and skill of the workers as they perform particular tasks on the meat as it crosses their paths on a conveyor belt.

Part 1
Mutton Chain 1; Mutton Chain 2; Mutton Chain 3; Beef Conveyor 1; Beef Conveyor 2; Stomach Removal.

Part 2
Boning Calves 1; Boning Beef 1; Boning Beef 2; Beef Conveyor 3; Beef Conveyor 1; Beef Conveyor 2; Stomach Removal.

The Video Show, Serpentine Gallery, 1975
(showed 12 mins of Mutton Chain).
Video V, Museum of Modern Art, New York, 1975
(showed 12 mins of Mutton Chain).
The Long Take, curated by Ron Brownson,
Auckland City Art Gallery, 1978.
Dauerleihagbe Ingrid Oppenhein, Städtisches Kunstmuseum
Bonn, 1983 (showed 10 mins of Mutton Chain 1, 10 mins of
Mutton Chain 2, and 10 mins of Boning).
Land Work People, Darcy Lange Survey,
Govett-Brewster Art Gallery, 1985.
*Lights>Camera>Action: Critical Moments from the
Govett-Brewster Collection 1969–2004*, curated by Simon Rees,
Govett-Brewster Art Gallery, 2004.
Viewfinder: Four Decades of the Govett-Brewster Art Collection,
Govett-Brewster Art Gallery, 2006.
Darcy Lange: Study of an Artist at Work,
Govett-Brewster Art Gallery, 2006.

Vern Hume, Aerial Top Dressing, Taranaki

Video, b/w photographs, sound, 47 mins.
Darcy Lange Estate and Govett-Brewster Art Gallery.
This work comprises documentation of Vern Hume, a top dresser in Taranaki, New Zealand. Lange recorded five trips from inside the aeroplane, each with a different angle of vision, three trips from the ground looking up at the plane, and one study of Hume having lunch along with a loader driver, a farmer, and Lange himself.

Work: study from aerial top dressing plane; study of plane doing circuit.
Personalisation: study of lunch break.

The Long Take, curated by Ron Brownson,
Auckland City Art Gallery, 1978.
Land Work People, Darcy Lange Survey,
Govett-Brewster Art Gallery, 1985.
Darcy Lange: Study of an Artist at Work,
Govett-Brewster Art Gallery, 2006.

Competition Axemen at Agricultural and Pastoral Show, Stratford, Taranaki

Video, b/w photographs, sound, 16 mins.
Darcy Lange Estate and Govett-Brewster Art Gallery.
Studies of a log-chopping competition and pastoral show in Stratford, New Zealand. Lange records the overhand chop, the underhand chop, and double-hand sawing competitions. These studies present the leisurely contest as work by centring on the physical exertions of the competitors.

Work: study of overhand chop; study of 12" underhand chop; study of 12" double-hand sawing.

The Long Take, curated by Ron Brownson,
Auckland City Art Gallery, 1978.
Land Work People, Darcy Lange Survey,
Govett-Brewster Art Gallery, 1985.
Darcy Lange: Study of an Artist at Work,
Govett-Brewster Art Gallery, 2006.

Bert Phillips, Study of a Fencer in Taranaki

Video. There are no known copies of this work.

Ruatoria, Study of Sheep Gathering and a Māori Shearing Gang, East Coast

Video, b/w photographs, sound, 161 mins.
Darcy Lange Estate and Govett-Brewster Art Gallery.
Studies of a Māori shearing gang recorded near Ruatoria, a small town in the North Island, and Māori-owned land. Lange makes studies of the farm manager and his stockman mustering and doing yard work, a shearing gang at work and during leisure time, and finally the family of the shearing contractor building a 'marae' (family meeting place).

Work: Muster (50 mins); Yard work (12 mins); Yard Work (12 mins); George Haig & Oli; Fleece-o (8 mins); Fleece-o (8 mins); Wool Press (10 mins); Shearing 'Pekama' (9 mins); Shearing 'Tim' (9 mins).
Personalisation: Walking from the Shed to the Cookhouse (5 mins); Meal Cookhouse (15 mins); Building New Marae Tuparoa Beach (20 mins); Shepherd's Children (3 mins).

The Video Show, Serpentine Gallery, London, 1975
(showed 12 mins of 'Portrait of Sydney').
Art Fair, Köln, 1975 (3 cassettes, 163 mins).
Video V, Museum of Modern Art, New York, 1975
(showed 12 mins of 'Portrait of Sydney').
The Long Take, curated by Ron Brownson,
Auckland City Art Gallery, 1978.
Dauerleihagbe Ingrid Oppenhein, Städtisches
Kunstmuseum Bonn, 1983 (3 cassettes, 163 mins).
Land Work People, Darcy Lange Survey,
Govett-Brewster Art Gallery, 1985.
Darcy Lange: Study of an Artist at Work,
Govett-Brewster Art Gallery, 2006.

1975
Cantavieja, Study of Work in a Spanish Village, Spain
Video, b/w photographs, sound, 44 mins.
Darcy Lange Estate and Govett-Brewster Art Gallery.
These are studies of people, in Cantavieja, (Maestrazgo, near Castellon, Spain) and the surrounding agricultural areas, performing various types of work: ploughing with tractors, cows, mules or bulls; scything wheat by hand; threshing wheat by machine; shepherding; and gathering greens for their domestic animals. These studies differ from the work made in New Zealand as they do not include the lunch break. The recordings were done over a week, but research covered five weeks. In the evening the video recordings were shown to the people who participated in them.

Part 1
Ploughing with Cows
Ploughing with Mules
Ploughing with Bulls
Scything Greens
Family Gathering Greens
Scything Wheat

Part 2
Wheat Gathering by Mule
The Village Harvester
Shepherdess

> *Land Work People, Darcy Lange Survey*,
> Govett-Brewster Art Gallery, 1985.
> *Darcy Lange: Study of an Artist at Work*,
> Govett-Brewster Art Gallery, 2006.
> *You and Me, Sometimes*, curated by Sandra Antelo-Suarez, Lehman Maupin Gallery, New York, 2008 (screening introduced by Dan Graham and Lori Zippay).

1976
Study of Three Birmingham Schools, UK
Video, b/w photographs, sound, approx. 6 hrs.
Darcy Lange Estate and Govett-Brewster Art Gallery.
This work focuses on the process of teaching and learning in the classroom. Lange chose institutions representative of different social classes and recorded the teaching of various subjects (English, mathematics, chemistry, physics, music, geography, biology and history). His intention was to study teaching and learning as work, while at the same time making a socio-economic comparison of teaching practices and their results. Moreover, in his comparison of subjects he wanted to display the creativity necessary to teach any subject: the arts and sciences alike. After the recordings, he invited students and teachers to view the tapes and comment on what they saw. He also taped the responses of two teachers. Three schools were selected for this series: Ladywood Comprehensive School, a racially mixed school in one of Birmingham's lowest income areas; King Edward's School, a privileged, boys only, public school where students are accepted based on academic merit; and Leabank Junior School, also a racially mixed school in a low income neighbourhood.

> Venice Biennale, 1976
> As *Teaching Studies* in *Dauerleihagbe Ingrid Oppenhein*, Städtisches Kunstmuseum Bonn, 1983 (60')
> *Land Work People, Darcy Lange Survey*, Govett-Brewster Art Gallery, 1985.
> *Darcy Lange: Study of an Artist at Work*, Govett-Brewster Art Gallery, 2006.

Film Studies in Comprehensive and Grammar Schools, UK
16 mm film, colour, sound. Darcy Lange Estate
These films are studies of a teacher's class, the teacher at home, and one of the students at home, and across different schools private and public following his comparative studies across class. This project is unfinished and parts have been lost. Only the following studies exist: Mr. Trott class study, Mr. Trott home study, and (student) Nicholas at home from King Edward's School; and Mis Kanta study class (no sound) from Ladywood Comprehensive School.

1977
Studies of Teaching in Four Oxfordshire Schools, UK
Video, b/w photographs, sound, approx. 6 hrs.
Darcy Lange Estate and Govett-Brewster Art Gallery.
This is a more structured further examination into the issue of teaching and learning as proposed the year before in the Birmingham schools project. In this case, Lange took four Oxfordshire schools as his subject. Again, he chose institutions representing different social classes, and also videotaped a wide range of subjects. For this project, he developed a structure focused on the comparison between the teaching of art/music, science, and history. As before, Lange videotaped the class study and played it back to his subjects, but in this instance he systematically recorded the students' and the teachers' responses to the tapes, incorporating them as part of the project to be exhibited. The practice of making his subjects into audience members not only questions the process of teaching, but also the effects of video. Lange resisted manipulation of the image, choosing long shots, zooming rarely and almost never moving the camera. He countered the techniques used by mass media to influence viewers, allowing the students and his larger audience to interpret the material on their own. The act of the students watching the class mirrors the participation Lange sought from his larger audience. He encouraged them to compare the various teachers, schools and

subjects, and invited them to question teaching as a socially constructive force. Unfortunately, parts of these studies have been lost.

Work Studies in Schools, curated by Mark Francis and commissioned by director David Elliott, Museum of Modern Art Oxford, 1977.
Land Work People, Darcy Lange Survey, Govett-Brewster Art Gallery, 1985.
Darcy Lange: Study of an Artist at Work, Govett-Brewster Art Gallery, 2006.

1977–80
Māori Land Project

Video. Darcy Lange Estate and Auckland Art Gallery Toi O Tamaki Collection.

In the early years of the Māori Renaissance, Pakeha (people of European descent) media activists joined the Māori people in their struggle to obtain and retain land rights. During these times, portable video served as a means to effect social change and organise communities. In this spirit, Lange began his work in 1997 on what then became *Māori Land Project*. In this project, he worked closely with photographer and Māori activist, John Miller, who often served either as cameraman or appeared in the footage. These recordings, which were made over a number of years, focus largely on two land cases: Ngatihine Block, north of Auckland, and Bastion Point in Auckland.

Ngatihine Block, 1977

Video, approx. 10 hrs. Darcy Lange Estate and Auckland Art Gallery Toi O Tamaki Collection.

Selection of video footage concerning issues regarding land rights as well as material specific to the Ngatihine Block case. The Ngatihine Block case was a legal battle to prevent Māori land from being leased by a forestry corporation. The corporation claimed their right to lease the land under the premise that it was poorly administrated and underdeveloped by the Māori owners.

Video Analysis – Māori Land Issue, Montevideo, Amsterdam, 27 March to 6 April 1978.
Het Land van de Māori, Van Abbemuseum, Eindhoven, 12 January to 10 February 1980.
Darcy Lange: Study of an Artist at Work, Govett-Brewster Art Gallery, 2006.

Bastion Point, 1977–80

Video, 144 mins. Darcy Lange Estate and Auckland Art Gallery Toi O Tamaki Collection.

These recordings of the Bastion Point case document the struggle over confiscated land that led to a confrontation between Māori and the New Zealand Government and police, and resulted in the incarceration of those who refused to leave the site. This case polarised New Zealand for over a year. In the Netherlands, Lange collaborated with René Coelho, director of Montevideo/

TBA in Amsterdam and Leonard Henny from Werkgroep Internationale Solidariteit, a centre in Utrecht dedicated to the research of media and its uses as a political tool. As a result of this collaboration, three projects were produced: a 25- minute piece for NOS Television, produced by Coelho; two versions of a 20 minute piece for a university research project by Henny and the Victor Jara Collective; and a much longer piece directed by Lange. A video was made in conjunction with the exhibition of Lange's *Māori Land Project* at the Internationaal Cultureel Centrum in Antwerp and the Van Abbemuseum in Eindhoven, introducing in Dutch subtitles basic facts about recent Māori history and Bastion Point.

Het Land van de Māori, Van Abbemuseum, Eindhoven, 12 January to 10 February 1980.
Dauerleihagbe Ingrid Oppenhein, Städtisches Kunstmuseum Bonn, 1983 (exhibited as *Takaparawha I*, 60 mins, *Takaparawha II* 60 mins, *Takaparawha III*, 60 mins.
Darcy Lange: Study of an Artist at Work, Govett-Brewster Art Gallery, 2006.

Russell Tribunal, 1980

Video, 120 mins. Darcy Lange Estate and Auckland City Art Gallery Toi O Tamaki Collection.

This is a recording of the Fourth Russell Tribunal celebrated in Rotterdam, the Netherlands on 25 November 1980. Although the conference focused on North American and South American indigenous issues, Lange was instrumental in bringing about the participation of the South Pacific people. This tape includes interventions by an Aboriginal Australian, an Eskimo from Greenland, Myron Mataoa from Tahiti representing Polynesia, and Colin Clark, spokesman for the Māori people of Aotearoa New Zealand.

Darcy Lange: Study of an Artist at Work, Govett-Brewster Art Gallery, 2006.

1983–4
People of the World

Multimedia opera, live music performance, video, slide projections. Darcy Lange Estate.

This project brought together 35 musicians from different countries – the Netherlands, Morocco, Spain, Greece, Turkey, Suriname and Indonesia – all with their own traditional folkloric roots, some even bearing similarities to flamenco. The musicians performed in front of a backdrop of slide projections and video. The project employed the traditional music of these immigrant groups in the Netherlands to counteract the alienation and marginalisation they suffered, and at the same time to foster a positive experience of sharing diverse cultural traditions. Rene Van Hoften from the Rasa Theatre in Holland was instrumental in this project. This work toured the Netherlands and eventually became a special UNESCO performance.

Land Work People, Darcy Lange Survey,
Govett-Brewster Art Gallery, 1985.
Darcy Lange: Study of an Artist at Work,
Govett-Brewster Art Gallery, 2006.

1986
Lack of Hope, Co-op a New Future
Video, 60 mins. Darcy Lange Estate
During the mid 1980s, as a result of the Labour Party's economic restructuring, New Zealand faced an increased unemployment rate. Lange conducted interviews with the unemployed, addressing the difficulties they faced dealing with, getting and keeping their social security benefits ('the dole'). The work addresses issues dealing with housing, health, race – as the underprivileged population was mostly Māori and Pacific Islanders – crime and education. It proposes rural communities or city economic 'co-ops' (co-operatives) as better, self-sustaining alternatives to state subsidy repression mechanisms such as the police or social welfare. This work was shown to alternative community groups.

Darcy Lange: Study of an Artist at Work,
Govett-Brewster Art Gallery, 2006.

A New Peace
A video installation with live performances by Darcy Lange, Maria Snijders, Denys Trussel and John Miller.

A New Peace, Artwork, Auckland, 11 to 22 August 1986.

1988–94
Aire del Mar
Multimedia opera, live music performance, video and slide projections. Darcy Lange Estate.
Following in the footsteps of *People of the World*, this multimedia project includes video, slide projections and live performances by Darcy Lange (flamenco guitar), Maria Snijders (flamenco guitar, singing, dancing, and choreography) and occasionally other performers and poets like Denys Trussel reading the poetry of Garcia Lorca. With a political subtext described as 'Land-Peace-People', it proposes a positive relationship with the environment. Projected on three screens, the slides presented an array of images celebrating nature, music and peace: of Aotearoa New Zealand and Andalusia's landscape, flamencos and fiestas, Goya's paintings and lithography from *The Disasters of War* and photographs and video stills of Lange's earlier works. Two monitors placed between the screens showed excerpts of Lange's videos, like *Cantavieja* or *Documentation of Bradford Working Life*, as characterising the rural and industrial realities of work, and the videos' sound added an aural backdrop to the live music.

Performed at Govett-Brewster Art Gallery; Sarjeant Art Gallery, Wanganui; City Art Gallery, Wellington; The Bath House, Rotorua; Artspace, Auckland, and the Maidment Theatre, University of Auckland, 1988.
Performed at the Maidment Theatre, University of Auckland, 1993.
Performed at the Gus Fisher Gallery, Auckland, 1994.
Darcy Lange: Study of an Artist at Work,
Govett-Brewster Art Gallery, 2006 (video documenting one of these performances).

1998–2000
Artists, Musicians and Poets at Work
Video, 30 mins each. Darcy Lange Estate.
A series of video portraits of New Zealand's leading artists, poets and musicians intended as a document of historical significance. In his Creative New Zealand application for funds to create these projects, Lange called these portraits a "kind of counter-television". In opposition to mass media techniques of excessive editing used in order to prevent audience boredom, Lange once again created portraits in 'real time'. He later showed these videos on the independent Triangle Television in Auckland. The series includes the artists Jim Allen, Don Binney, Philippa Blair, Graham Brett, Barry Brickell, Ted Bulmore, Len Castle, Phil Dadson, Robert Ellis, Ralph Hotere, Alyson Hunter, Alexis Hunter, Rick Killeen, Ian Macdonald, Marianne Muggeridge, Keith Patterson, Claudia Pond Eyley, Ross Ritchie, Ken Robinson, Michael Smither, Greer Twiss, Robin White, Arnold Wilson and Maria Shannon; musicians Ruri Sunde, Paco Campana (Lange's flamenco music name) and Alan Muggeridge; and poet Denys Trussel.

Darcy Lange: Study of an Artist at Work,
Govett-Brewster Art Gallery, 2006.

Selected Bibliography

Books and Catalogues

Mercedes Vicente (ed.), *Darcy Lange: Study of an Artist at Work*, essays by Guy Brett, Benjamin H. D. Buchloh, Dan Graham, Lawrence McDonald, John Miller and Geraldene Peters, Pedro G. Romero and Mercedes Vicente, Govett-Brewster Art Gallery, New Plymouth, New Zealand and Ikon, Birmingham, United Kingdom, 2008.

Mercedes Vicente, 'Work Studies in Schools', *Documenta 12 Magazine No. 3: Education:*, (eds.) Schöllhammer, Georg/Buergel, Roger M./Noack, Ruth, Taschen, 2007.

Darcy Lange Video Art, The Department of Film, Television and Media Studies, University of Auckland, Auckland 2001.

Dauerleihagbe Ingrid Oppenhein, Städtisches Kunstmuseum Bonn, 1983 (exhibition catalogue).

Het Land van de Māori, Māori Land Project, Stedelijk Van Abbemuseum, Eindhoven and Internationaal Cultureel Centrum, Antwerp 1980 (exhibition catalogue).

Lives, Hayward Gallery, London 1979 (exhibition catalogue).

Work Studies in Schools, Museum of Modern Art Oxford, Oxford 1977 (exhibition catalogue).

La Biennale di Venezia, Vol. 2, 1976, p. 344 (exhibition catalogue).

9e Biennale de Paris à Nice, Direction des Musées de Nice, Nice 1976 (exhibition catalogue).

9e Biennale de Paris, 1975 (exhibition catalogue).

Artists' Video Tapes, Palais Des Beaux-Arts, Brussels 1975 (exhibition catalogue).

6th Mildura Sculpture Exhibition, Mildura, Victoria, Australia, 1975 (exhibition catalogue).

The Video Show, Serpentine Gallery, London 1975 (exhibition catalogue).

Six New Zealand Artists, Antoinette Godkin, Auckland City Art Gallery 1974 (exhibition catalogue).

Wulf Herzogenrath, Projekt '74, *Aspekte Internationaler Kunst am Anfang der 70er Jahre*, Köln 1974 (exhibition catalogue).

A Survey of the Avant-Garde in Britain, Gallery House, London 1972, (exhibition catalogue).

Articles and Reviews

Mercedes Vicente, 'Work Studies in Schools', David Hatcher (ed.), *Natural Selection Magazine* (www.naturalselection.org.nz), #6, 2007, p.9.

Lawrence McDonald 'A Life's Work: Darcy Lange in Retrospect', *Illusions* #39, winter 2007, p. 40.

Jo Smith, 'Reciprocal Respect: Darcy Lange's Video Art in the Context of New Media', *Illusions* #39, winter 2007, p. 44.

Mark Amery, 'Lange's Work Comes Full Circle', *The Dominion Post*, 20 April 2007, p. B9.

Martin Rumsby, 'Darcy Lange: Study of an Artist at Work' *Art New Zealand* #121, summer 2006, p. 76.

Aaron Kreisler, 'Rewind', *Listener*, 29 September 2006, p. 46.

Jonathan Dennis and Jan Bieringa (eds.) *Film in Aotearoa New Zealand*, Victoria University of Wellington Press, Wellington 1992, p. 64.

Auckland Star, 6 October 1988.

New Zealand Herald, 29 September 1988, section 2, p. 5.

'Real Pictures Moves into Video Market', *Auckland City Harbour News*, 30 July 1986.

'Time Now for Video Art Gallery', *Auckland Star*, 23 July 1986.

Tom Hutchins 'The Flamingo and the Bomb: A Performance by Darcy and Miriam Lange', *Art New Zealand*, autumn 1988, #50, p. 38.

Dan Graham, 'Darcy Lange: Work and Music', *New Observations*, #29, 1985.

New Zealand Art News, April/May 1985, p. 28.

'Photographic Art in Many Forms', *The Dominion*,
17 April 1985.

'Artist's Creativity Turns People's Actions into Art',
Taranaki Herald, 6 April 1985.

'Video Art Features in Exhibition', *Taranaki Herald*,
30 March 1985.

'Review: Darcy Lange', *Video Art*, April/May 1980.

Video Art, November 1978/January 1979, p. 17.

'Angel Mine', *Craccum*, 18 September 1978.

'Bastion Point', *Craccum*, 17 April 1978, p. 7.

'The Last Bastion Point', *Craccum*, vol. 52, #10, 1978.

'Out for a Stroll', *New Plymouth Daily News*,
28 October 1977.

Darcy Lange and Andrew Turner, Industrial Museum,
Bradford Art Galleries and Museums, Bradford, 1976.

'Video Studies 1975 and 1976', *Studio International*,
May/June 1976, p. 191.

'Narrow Focus in an Empty Gallery', *Australian*,
19 September 1975.

'Darcy Lange: A Conversation with Willoughby Sharp',
Avalanche (New York), summer 1975, p. 12.

'Video Show', *Art & Artists*, May 1975, p. 24.

'Weird and Wonderful', *Evening Post*, 16 December 1974.

'Expatriates Point Way to an Upright Stance',
Auckland Star, 7 September 1974.

'Seeing Eyes for Six', *New Zealand Listener*,
28 September 1974.

'Sculptors of Talent but are they Kiwi Artists?',
The Sunday Herald, 1 September 1974.

'Six New Zealand Artists', *Auckland Star*, 26 August 1974.

'Avant-garde Show by Six New Zealand Artists',
The New Zealand Herald, 24 August 1974.

Guy Brett 'In Exhibition at New Zealand House',
The Times, London, 20 February 1973, p. 5.

'London Show for Six New Zealand Artists',
The New Zealand Herald, 14 February 1973.

Rosetta Brooks 'Darcy Lange at the Jack Wendler Gallery',
Studio International, spring 1973, p.109.

'Sculpture to Feature', *The Waikato Times*, 28 August 1971.

'Architectural D'Arcy', *Craccum Art Supplement*,
2 September 1968.

'Formality Keynote', *Auckland Star*, 4 September 1968.

'Bought for Art Gallery', *Taranaki Herald*, 30 May 1968.

'To Study at Royal College', *Taranaki Herald*, 17 May 1968.

'Variety is the Big Thing About Sculpture Show',
Auckland Star, 23 November 1967.

'Sculpture Display Excellent', *New Zealand Herald*,
21 November 1967.

'Stimulating Display of Local Sculpture', *Auckland Star*,
5 December 1966.

'Sculpture Display Full of Life', *New Zealand Herald*,
30 November 1966.

'As It Is – And As It Was', *Auckland Star*,
11 November, 1966, p. 7.

'Scrap Art', *Auckland Star*, 12 October 1966, p. 71.

Acknowledgements

Mercedes Vicente

This publication has been a work in progress for over two years. It was to accompany the 2006 retrospective exhibition *Darcy Lange: Study of an Artist at Work*, organised by the Govett-Brewster Art Gallery, but grew in scale and ambition alongside the archival efforts of the larger Darcy Lange project. It is pleasing that this publication has now coincided with the exhibition *Work Studies in Schools* at Ikon Gallery in Birmingham, and is co-published with Ikon. I would like to thank Rhana Devenport, Director, Govett-Brewster Art Gallery and Jonathan Watkins, Director, Ikon Gallery for their vision in recognising the relevance of this project. My special gratitude is extended to Helen Legg, co-curator of the Ikon exhibition, for sharing her brilliant observations, her enthusiasm and her dedicated research into this important body of work by Lange.

I would like to warmly thank the authors Guy Brett, Benjamin H. D. Buchloh, Dan Graham, John Miller, Geraldene Peters, Lawrence McDonald and Pedro G. Romero for their insightful and thought-provoking essays, and for the tireless research they have conducted in order to pay their respects to Lange's legacy. Special thanks to Allan Sekula for his keen engagement throughout.

I would also like to acknowledge the dedication and diligence of Helen Telford, Assistant Director, Govett-Brewster Art Gallery for her co-ordination of this publication. My sincere gratitude goes to Alejandra Rojas, who curatorially assisted me in the early stages of the 2006 retrospective and was able to come on board in the last steps of this publication, compiling the Chronology and List of Works. I am in debt to her for her insightful contribution and relentless commitment to this project. Special thanks as well to Fiona Moorhead for her invaluable support in the early stages of the formation of the Darcy Lange Archive, and with whom I share memorable moments and findings. My gratitude goes to Andrew Clark for his generous assistance as intern for the Darcy Lange Archive and for his early input for the Chronology, I sincerely appreciate his commitment. Heartfelt thanks to Courtney Lucas for her generous and tremendous efforts in cataloguing and compiling Lange's photographic archive, and for her keen photographic eye as photo editor of this book. Very special thanks to those who made available for reproduction their photography: Bryan James, Bill Davidson and John Miller. I am also grateful to David Auerbach for his thorough and fine translation of Pedro G. Romero's essay and to Susette Goldsmith, copy editor, for her attentive care and accommodating attitude. Thanks to James Langdon for designing this beautiful publication and to Kalee Jackson, Govett-Brewster designer, for her earlier design assistance and support for the project.

No exhibition can be achieved without the dedicated assistance of the whole gallery staff. I would like to extend my gratitude to the Govett-Brewster Art Gallery team for their professionalism and commitment to the 2006 retrospective: to Kate Roberts, former Acting Director for her support in this project; to Bryan James, Exhibitions Co-ordinator for his meticulous care in mounting exhibitions, and for the co-ordination of his dedicated installation team of Anton Berndt, Duncan Carter, Kevin Castle, Cameron Curd, Michael Parr, Bruce E. Phillips and Leonie Smith; to our Registrar Amanda Ward for enthusiastically tracking down Lange's early sculptures and supervising their restoration; Claire Blackman and Cressida Gates who oversaw marketing and publicity respectively; to our education team Chris Barry and Rebecca Fawkner-Egli for implanting the seeds of inspiration in our younger audiences; to Bronwyn Van't Hof and our wonderful Information Officers team: Duncan Carter, Therese O'Connell, Fiona Moorhead, Justin Morgan, Paula Newton, Leonie Smith and Bruce E. Phillips, whose work with the public has been invaluable; and last our retirees, Joanne Cuthbert for her tremendous work with the gallery's Foundation, and Angela Park for assisting in all administrative matters.

I must emphasise the immense assistance of the New Zealand Film Archive – Frank Stark and his staff, particularly Jamie Lean and Geoff Rogers, and Bruce Anderson and Virginia Callanan, who allocated endless hours of viewing, cataloguing and mastering of tapes, working around the clock under great pressure to deliver on time the works presented in the 2006 retrospective and in the current exhibition at Ikon. This has been a collaboration that continues with the on-going archival efforts toward Lange's entire oeuvre now deposited in the archive.

Many other individuals and organisations have also provided support. I am in debt to a long list of artists, scholars and critics, as well as family and friends whom I contacted in my research including: Aaron Kreisler, Abigail Gampel, Abina Manning, Andrew Clifford, Antoinette Godkin, Barbara London, Blake Stimson, Bob Ellis, Boyd Webb, Bruce Ralston, Caroline McBride,

Catherine Hammond, Charlotte Huddleston, Cody Trepte, David Bornstein, David Elliott, David Hatcher, Debra Singer, Elise MacDonald, Euridice Arratia, Fiona Clark, Gary Cann, Greg Burke, Gwyneth Porter, Henriette Huldisch, Ian MacDonald, Jack Wendler, Jan Bieringa, Jim Allen, John Baldessari, John Eagles, John Maynard, John McCormack, Jon Bywater, Kasper König, Leon Narbey, Leonhard Emerling, Leslie Downing, Leslie Kreisler, Linda Taylor, Lori Zippay, Louise Cann, Luit Bieringa, Martin Rumsby, Muntadas, Newton Lange, Natasha Conland, Norie Neumark, Paul Minifie, Peggy Gale, Peter Grove, Phil Dadson, Phil Slight, Phillip Allen, René Block, Rodney Wilson, Roger Conover, Roger Horrocks, Ron Brownson, Rosetta Brooks, Sabrina Guadagnino, Sandra Antelo-Suarez, Sandra Firmin, Shirley Horrocks, Sue Crockford, Susanne Jaschko, Tomas Eller, Walther König, Warren Olds, William McAloon, Willoughby Sharp, Wulf Herzogenrath and Wystan Curnow.

I am most thankful to Christina Barton, a friend and colleague, for her steadfast support and trust in this project from its early stages, and for the invitation to host the 2006 retrospective at Adam Art Gallery in its inaugural exhibition under her new direction. I would also like to warmly thank my friend and colleague John Di Stefano for his wisdom and loyal friendship (and for offering a home for my many trips to Wellington to conduct research at the New Zealand Film Archive). Many thanks to Tyler Cann, Len Lye Curator at the gallery, with whom I have shared many moments during the development of this project, for his wonderful disposition and generous insightful inputs. My most special thanks go to Peter R. Wareing for his inspiring and most devoted appreciation of the efforts involved in bringing to term this project.

This publication was made possible through a significant grant from Creative New Zealand. Special thanks to Jude Chambers for her guidance and support, and to Melanie Oliver, Assistant Curator, for her tremendous tenacity in the grant writing application. The early support of Taranaki Electricity Trust also was crucial and deeply appreciated; I would like to especially thank Fiona Clark in this regard. And I am grateful to the Govett-Brewster Foundation for financial support and for recognising the value and importance of this publication.

And finally, I am most appreciative to Lange's children Darcy and Rawinia, the beneficiaries of the Darcy Lange Estate, as well as Maria, Lange's former wife, for their trust placed in this project and their invaluable support. And I thank Lange's brother Roger, for his kind assistance in retrieving the Darcy Lange Archive. My relationship with them all has added a tremendous human dimension to the project, for which I am most grateful.

Acknowledgements

Contributors' Biographies

Guy Brett lives and works in London. He has written for the art press since the 1960s and has organised a number of international exhibitions. He is a member of the advisory board of *Third Text* and is Visiting Professor at the University of the Arts, London. His books include *Kinetic Art* (1968), *Through Our Own Eyes: Popular Art and Modern History* (1986), *Transcontinental: Nine Latin American Artists* (1990), *Exploding Galaxies: The Art of David Medalla* (1995), *Carnival of Perception* (2004) and *Brasil Experimental: Arte/Vida Proposições e Paradoxos* (2005).

Benjamin H. D. Buchloh is Andrew W. Mellon Professor of Modern and Contemporary Art at Harvard University. He is one of the editors of *October* magazine, and is the author, jointly with Hal Foster, Yve-Alain Bois and Rosalind Krauss of *Art Since 1900* (2002). More recently he has published essays on Gerhard Richter, Raymond Pettibon and Andy Warhol. The second volume of his collected essays, entitled *Formalism and Historicity* will be published in 2009.

Dan Graham is an artist based in New York. He is an influential figure in the field of contemporary art, as practitioner, critic and theorist. His artistic practice includes film, video, performance, photography and architecture. Graham's writings have been published in many magazines and publications, among the most significant are *Two Way Mirror Power: Selected Writings by Dan Graham on His Art*, *Half Square Half Crazy*, and *Sympathy for the Devil: Art and Rock and Roll Since 1967*.

Lawrence McDonald is a writer, editor, curator, and lecturer based in Wellington. He is editor of the publications *Les Cleveland: Six Decades – Message from the Exterior* (1998) and *Handboek: Ans Westra Photographs* (2004), and *Illusions*, a journal of moving image and performing arts criticism. He teaches in the Department of Art History, Victoria University of Wellington. In 1999, he curated *PALeo Neo Video: Chapters from the History of Video Art in New Zealand 1970s – 1990s*, which featured the work of Darcy Lange.

John Miller is a documentary photographer, of the Ngaitewake-ki-uta, Uritaniwha and Ngati Rehia hapū of Ngapuhi, from the far north of the North Island. Since the late 1960s he has photographed political, social and cultural events and is well known for his documentation of the Māori Renaissance. Miller collaborated with Darcy Lange during the Ngatihine Maori land dispute and again in 1986 on a project shot around the East Coast of the North Island. He also videotaped Lange's final series of flamenco concerts. In 2003, Miller was awarded a New Zealand Media Peace Prize lifetime achievement award.

Dr. Geraldene Peters is senior lecturer in Media Studies at Auckland University of Technology, researching documentary studies, alternative/community media, visual culture and moving image history in Aotearoa/New Zealand. Most recently, she has published on the work of filmmaker Merata Mita, the documentary *Patu!*, the left-wing film collective Vanguard Films, and the work of video artist Jayce Salloum. Since the early 1990s she has worked as researcher, production manager and assistant editor across a range of documentary projects from community video to international films.

Pedro G. Romero is an artist based in Seville, Spain. Since the late 1990s he has worked on two projects: Archivo F.X. and Máquina P.H. He is member of Plataforma de Reflexión de Políticas Culturales and the contents team for Art and Thought at the Universidad Internacional de Andalucia. His latest projects include *La Ciudad Vacía: Comunidad* (2005–7) as part of Archivo F.X., commissioned by Fundació Antoni Tàpies, Barcelona and exhibited in *Heterotopias* (2007), curated by Catherine David. As part of Máquina P.H., he has directed *Arena* (2004), *Tabula Rasa* (2006) and *El Final de este Estado de Cosas* (2007) with the flamenco dancer Israel Galván. Romero co-curated, with Patricia Molins, the exhibition *La Noche Española, Flamenco, Vanguardia y Cultura Popular 1865–1936* (2007) at the Museo Nacional Reina Sofia, Madrid.

Mercedes Vicente is Curator at the Govett-Brewster Art Gallery. She earned an MA in Film and the Arts at New York University and Curatorial Studies at Bard College and was Helena Rubinstein Curatorial Fellow at the Whitney Independent Study Program. Her most recent exhibitions include: *From Mini-FM to Hacktivists: A Guide to Art and Activism* (2005); *Darcy Lange: Study of an Artist at Work* (2006); *Activating Korea: Tides of Collective Action* (2007), with INSA Art Space, Seoul. She is co-curator, with Helen Legg, of *Darcy Lange: Work Studies in Schools* (2008) at Ikon. Vicente has contributed to many publications and written on Louise Bourgeois, Andrea Fraser and Martha Rosler.

Darcy Lange: Study of an Artist at Work
29 July to 24 September 2006

Govett-Brewster Art Gallery
42 Queen Street
Private Bag 2025
New Plymouth 4340, New Zealand
Tel. +64 6 759 6060
Fax. +64 6 758 0390
www.govettbrewster.com

Director
Rhana Devenport (from September 2006)

Acting Director
Kate Roberts (to September 2006)

Curator
Mercedes Vicente

Exhibition Coordination
Bryan James

Exhibition Installation
Anton Berndt, Duncan Carter, Kevin Castle,
Cameron Curd, Michael Parr, Bruce E. Phillips,
Leonie Smith

Registration
Amanda Ward

Designer
Kalee Jackson

Marketing and Administration
Clare Blackman, Cressida Gates, Angela Parr

Education
Chris Barry, Rebecca Fawkner-Egli

Information Services
Bronwyn van't Hof, Duncan Carter, Therese O'Connell,
Fiona Moorhead, Justin Morgan, Paula Newton,
Leonie Smith, Bruce E. Phillips

Exhibition supported by Creative New Zealand and with
the assistance of The New Zealand Film Archive

Govett-Brewster Art Gallery is principally funded
by New Plymouth District Council

Darcy Lange Work Studies in Schools
26 November 2008 to 25 January 2009

Ikon Gallery
1 Oozells Square
Brindleyplace
Birmingham
B1 2HS, UK
Tel. +44 121 248 0708
www.ikon-gallery.co.uk

Curated by Helen Legg and Mercedes Vicente

Director
Jonathan Watkins

Deputy Director
Judith Harry

Curators
Nigel Prince, Helen Legg

Exhibition Coordination
Sarah McAlister

Programme Assistant
Alexandra Lockett

Exhibition Installation
Matt Nightingale, Chris Maggs, Richard Short,
Sudhir Khimji

Marketing and Administration
Rebecca Small, Jigisha Patel, Emily Luxford

Education
Kaija Kaitavuori, Emma Bowen, James Cangiano,
Nikki Shaw

IT/AV Manager
Matthew Hogan

Ikon gratefully acknowledges financial assistance
from Arts Council England, West Midlands and
Birmingham City Council

ISBN: 9781904864509

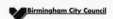

Editor
Mercedes Vicente

Publication Coordinator
Helen Telford

Contributors
Guy Brett, Benjamin H. D. Buchloh, Dan Graham,
John Miller, Geraldene Peters, Lawrence McDonald,
Pedro G. Romero, Mercedes Vicente

Additional contributions for the Chronology and
List of Works by Alejandra Rojas and Andrew Clark

Translator
David Auerbach

Copy Editor
Susette Goldsmith

Designer
James Langdon

Photography
Bryan James, Ian MacDonald, John Miller

Photo Editor
Courtney Lucas

Darcy Lange Archive Assistants
Andrew Clark, Courtney Lucas, Fiona Moorhead

Distributed by Cornerhouse in all countries
but Australia and New Zealand

Cornerhouse
70 Oxford Street
Manchester
M1 5NH, UK
Tel. +44 161 228 7621